THE MODERN **KNIT** MIX

Neck Effects

30 SCARVES, WRAPS, & COWLS

TO **KNIT** FOR NOW

THE MODERN **KNIT** MIX

Neck Effects

30 SCARVES, WRAPS, & COWLS TO **KNIT** FOR NOW

FEATURING **CASCADE YARNS® HERITAGE**

 sixth&springbooks NEW YORK

sixth&spring books

161 Avenue of the Americas, New York, NY 10013
sixthandspringbooks.com

Managing Editor
LAURA COOKE

Senior Editor
LISA SILVERMAN

Art Director
DIANE LAMPHRON

Supervising Patterns Editor
CARLA SCOTT

Yarn Editor
VANESSA PUTT

Patterns Editors
PAT HARSTE
RENEE LORION
LORI STEINBERG

Photography
RON GOODGER

Fashion Stylist
STAN WILLIAMS

Hair & Makeup
ANNIE VAN DYKE

Vice President
TRISHA MALCOLM

Publisher
CAROLINE KILMER

Production Manager
DAVID JOINNIDES

President
ART JOINNIDES

Chairman
JAY STEIN

This book was created in collaboration with Quarto Publishing Group USA.

Library of Congress Cataloging-in-Publication Data
Neck effects : 30 scarves, wraps, and cowls to knit for now featuring cascade yarns heritage / the editors of Sixth&Spring Books. — 1st [edition].
     pages cm
ISBN 978-1-936096-90-9
1. Knitting—Patterns. 2. Neckwear. I. Sixth & Spring Books.
TT825.N364 2015
746.43'2041—dc23
                                        2015006200

Manufactured in China

1 3 5 7 9 10 8 6 4 2

First Edition

Contents

INTRODUCTION
Neck and Neck…and Neck 7

Neck and Neck . . . and Neck

If you're a knitter, chances are you like to knit neckwear. Beginners start with a simple rectangular scarf or cowl, and as skills expand, large shawls and complex stitch patterns enter the picture. Neckwear often features simple construction and minimal shaping, making it the perfect canvas for a multitude of techniques—whether you're learning something new or looking to enjoy your favorite style of knitting. And since fit isn't an issue, neckwear is the quintessential knitted gift!

In these pages you'll find 30 unique, modern designs for scarves, cowls, and shawls, all knit in Cascade Yarns' Heritage line: Heritage, Heritage Paints, Heritage Silk, and Heritage Silk Paints. These fingering-weight superwash merino blends are soft and easy to care for, and come in a multitude of vibrant colorways. Heritage is perfect for everything from lace to cables to colorwork—and you'll find beautiful examples of each, suited to every skill level.

Whether you're a northerner who can't have too many cozy winter accessories, or live in a warm climate and love lacy scarves and shawls, the designs in this book are an essential addition to your knitting library.

Projects

Wilma

DESIGNED BY LORETTA DACHMAN

A chevron pattern formed with only knit and purl stitches is easy to work
but looks luxurious knit in a variegated colorway.

FINISHED MEASUREMENTS
Circumference 38"/96.5cm
Length 9"/23cm

MATERIALS
- One 3½oz/100g hank (each approx 437yd/400m) of Cascade Yarns *Heritage Silk Paints* (superwash merino wool/mulberry silk) in #9801 fall foliage 🌀 Slight variations in color can occur with handpainted yarns, and can occur between dye lots.
- Size 5 (3.75mm) circular needle, 24"/60cm long, *or size to obtain gauge*
- Stitch marker

GAUGE
25 sts and 42 rows to 4"/10cm over chevron pat using size 5 (3.75mm) needle.
Take time to check gauge.

CHEVRON PATTERN
(multiple of 12 sts)
Rnd 1 *K1, p2, k2, p1; rep from * around.
Rnd 2 *P2, k2; rep from * around.
Rnd 3 *P1, k2, p2, k1; rep from * around.
Rnd 4 *K2, p2; rep from * around.
Rep rnds 1–4 for chevron pat.

NOTE
Chevron pattern can be worked from text OR chart.

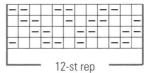

12-st rep

STITCH KEY

☐ k on RS, p on WS

⊟ p on RS, k on WS

COWL
Cast on 240 sts. Join, being careful not to twist sts, and place marker for beg of rnd. Rep rnds 1–4 of chevron pat until cowl measures 9"/23cm. Bind off purlwise. ■

Harper

DESIGNED BY FELICITY THOMAS

A modern Fair Isle block pattern framed by garter stitch edges
makes a striking unisex scarf.

FINISHED MEASUREMENTS
Approx 7 x 63"/18 x 160cm

MATERIALS
- One 3½oz/100g hank (each approx 437yd/400m)
  of Cascade Yarns *Heritage* (superwash merino
  wool/nylon) each in #5603 marine (A) and #5656
  Christmas green (B)
- One pair size 3 (3.25mm) needles *or size to
  obtain gauge*

GAUGE
36 sts and 32 rows to 4"/10cm over color pat 1 using
size 3 (3.25mm) needles.
Take time to check gauge.

COLOR PAT 1
(multiple of 7 sts plus 2, plus 6 border sts)
Row 1 (WS) With A, k3, p to last 3 sts, k3.
Rows 2 and 4 K5 A, *k5 B, k2 A; rep from * to last
3 sts, k3.
Rows 3 and 5 K3 A, *p2 A, p5 B; rep from * to last 5
sts; with A, p2, k3.
Row 6 With A, knit.
Rep rows 1–6 for color pat 1.

COLOR PAT 2
(multiple of 7 sts plus 2, plus 6 border sts)
Row 1 (WS) With B, k3, p to last 3 sts, k3.
Rows 2 and 4 K5 B, *k5 A, k2 B; rep from *

to last 3 sts, k3.
Rows 3 and 5 K3 B, *p2 B, p5 A; rep from * to last 5
sts; with B, p2, k3.
Row 6 With B, knit.
Rep rows 1–6 for color pat 2.

SCARF
With A, cast on 57 sts.
Knit 1 (RS) row.
Begin color pats
[Rep rows 1–6 of color pat 1 for 14 times, rep rows
1–6 of color pat 2 for 14 times] three times. Break A.
Next row (WS) With B, k3, p to last 3 sts, k3.
Bind off.

FINISHING
Block gently if necessary. ■

Victoria

DESIGNED BY LYNN M. WILSON

A cozy neckwarmer, worked in the round and shaped by changing needle sizes, combines zigzag lace and a snug ribbed collar.

■ ■ ■ ■▶

FINISHED MEASUREMENTS
Lower edge circumference 22"/56cm
Neck circumference (unstretched) 14"/35.5cm
Length (not folded) 12"/30.5cm

MATERIALS
- One 3½oz/100g hank (each approx 437yd/400m) of Cascade Yarns *Heritage* (superwash merino wool/nylon) in #5636 sapphire (❶)
- One each sizes 4, 5, and 6 (3.5, 3.75, and 4mm) circular needles, 16"/40cm long, *or size to obtain gauge*
- Stitch marker

GAUGES
23 sts and 32 rows to 4"/10cm over St st using size 4 (3.5mm) needle.
18 sts and 31 rnds after blocking to 4"/10cm over St st using size 6 (4mm) needle.
Take time to check gauges.

LACE PATTERN
(multiple of 7 sts)
Rnds 1–12 *K2, yo, k1, yo, k2tog tbl, k2tog; rep from * around.
Rnds 13–24 *K2, k2tog tbl, k2tog, yo, k1, yo; rep from * around.
Rep rnds 1–24 for lace pat.

RIB PATTERN
(multiple of 7 sts)
Rnd 1 K2, p4, *k3, p4; rep from * to last st, k1.
Rep rnd 1 for rib pat.

NOTE
Cowl is worked from lower edge to ribbed collar.

COWL
With size 6 (4mm) needle, cast on 98 sts. Join, being careful not to twist sts, and place marker for beg of rnd.
Purl 1 rnd.

Begin lace pat
Work rnds 1–12 of lace pat.
Change to size 5 (3.75mm) needle. Work rnds 13–24 of lace pat.
Change to size 4 (3.5mm) needle. Work rnds 1–24 of lace pat once, then rep rnds 1–12 once more.

Begin rib pat
Work in rib pat for 3"/7.5cm. Change to size 5 (3.75mm) needle.
Cont in rib pat for 5 rnds more. Change to size 6 (4mm) needle.
Cont in rib pat for 4 rnds more. Bind off loosely in pat.

FINISHING
Block to open lace, avoiding ribbing. ■

Elizabeth

DESIGNED BY LIDIA KARABINECH

A garter stitch base adds structure to a versatile, ethereal scarf
with an allover zigzag lace pattern.

FINISHED MEASUREMENTS
Approx 12¼ x 64"/31 x 162.5cm after blocking

MATERIALS
- Two 3½oz/100g hanks (each approx 437yd/400m)
  of Cascade Yarns *Heritage* (superwash merino
  wool/nylon) in #5618 snow 🔳
- One pair size 5 (3.75mm) needles *or size to
  obtain gauge*

GAUGE
24 sts and 30 rows to 4"/10cm after blocking over
lace pat using size 5 (3.75mm) needles.
Take time to check gauge.

LACE PATTERN
(multiple of 8 sts)
Row 1 (RS) *K6, k2tog, yo; rep from * to end.
Row 2 (WS) *K1, yo, p2tog, k5; rep from * to end.
Row 3 *K4, k2tog, yo, k2, rep from * to end.
Row 4 *K3, yo, p2tog, k3, rep from * to end.
Row 5 *K2, k2tog, yo, k4, rep from * to end.
Row 6 *K5, yo, p2tog, k1, rep from * to end.
Row 7 *K2tog, yo, k6, rep from * to end.
Row 8 *K6, p2tog tbl, yo, rep from * to end.
Row 9 *K1, yo, ssk, k5, rep from * to end.
Row 10 *K4, p2tog tbl, yo, k2, rep from * to end.
Row 11 *K3, yo, ssk, k3, rep from * to end.
Row 12 *K2, p2tog tbl, yo, k4, rep from * to end.
Row 13 *K5, yo, ssk, k1, rep from * to end.
Row 14 *P2tog tbl, yo, k6, rep from * to end.
Rep rows 1–14 for lace pat.

NOTES
1) Lace pat can be worked from text OR chart.
2) First and last st of every row are worked in
garter st.

SCARF
Cast on 74 sts. Knit 2 rows.

Begin lace pat
Row 1 (RS) K1, work 8-st rep 9 times across, k1.
Row 2 (WS) K1, work 8-st rep 9 times across, k1.
Cont in this manner until row 14 of lace pat is
complete. Rep rows 1–14 until scarf measures
64"/162.5cm from beg. Knit 2 rows. Bind off loosely.

FINISHING
Block to maximum size to open lace. ◼

LACE PAT

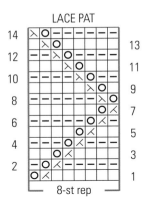

8-st rep

STITCH KEY

☐ k on RS, p on WS

⊟ p on RS, k on WS

◿ k2tog on RS, p2tog on WS

◺ ssk on RS, P2tog tbl on WS

◎ yo

Isadora

DESIGNED BY JACQUELINE VAN DILLEN

A slip stitch color pattern is beautifully bookended by the two colors used alone in fringe and in a unique style of ribbing.

FINISHED MEASUREMENTS
Approx 7 x 67"/18 x 170cm

MATERIALS
- One 3½oz/100g hank (each approx 437yd/400m) of Cascade Yarns *Heritage* (superwash merino wool/nylon) each in #5610 camel (A) and #5630 anis (B) 🧶❶
- One pair size 3 (3.25mm) needles *or size to obtain gauge*
- Size G/6 (4mm) crochet hook for fringe

GAUGE
26 sts and 56 rows to 4"/10cm over slip st color pat using size 3 (3.25mm) needles.
Take time to check gauge.

FANTASIE RIB
(multiple of 4 sts plus 1)
Row 1 (RS) *K2, k1 wrapping yarn twice around

needle, k1; rep from * to last st, k1.
Row 2 *K2, p1 dropping extra wrap, k1; rep from * to last st, k1.
Rep rows 1 and 2 for fantasie rib.

SLIP STITCH COLOR PATTERN
(multiple of 12 sts plus 1)
Rows 1, 5, 9, and 13 (RS) With A, knit.
Rows 2, 6, 10, and 14 With A, purl.
Row 3 With B, sl 2, *p9, sl 3; rep from * to last 10 sts, p9, sl 1.
Row 4 With B, sl 1, *k9, sl 3; rep from * to last 11 sts, k9, sl 2.
Row 7 With B, *p1, sl 3, p5, sl 3; rep from * to end.
Row 8 With B, *sl 3, k5, sl 3; rep from *, end k1.
Row 11 With B, *p3, sl 3, p1, sl 3, p2; rep from * to end.
Row 12 With B, *k2, sl 3, k1, sl 3, k3; rep from *, end k1.
Row 15 With B, p5, sl 3, *p9, sl 3; rep from * to last 4 sts, p4.
Row 16 With B, k4, *sl 3, k9; rep from * to last 8 sts, sl 3, k5.

NOTES
1) Slip sts purlwise with yarn to the WS of piece.
2) Piece is worked with selvedge sts throughout.

SCARF
With A, cast on 51 sts.
Next row (RS) Sl 1 purlwise (selvedge), work row 1 of fantasie rib to last st, k1 (selvedge st).
Next row Sl 1 knitwise (selvedge), work row 2 of fantasie rib to last st, p1 (selvedge).
Cont in this way, working selvedge sts at each end and rep rows 1 and 2 of fantasie rib until piece measures 4½"/11.5cm from beg.

Begin slip st color pat
Cont to work selvedge sts at each end, work in slip st color pat until piece measures approx 56"/142cm from beg. With A, work in fantasie rib for 4½"/11.5cm more. Bind off.

FINISHING
Fringe
Cut 156 strands of B, each 8"/20.5cm long. Holding 6 strands tog, fold in half, forming a loop. With crochet hook, draw the loop through a stitch in one end of scarf. Draw the ends of the strands through the loop and pull tight. Rep evenly along both ends of scarf (13 fringe in each end). ■

Joan

DESIGNED BY WEI WILKINS

A lace panel shaped by varying needle sizes is seamed into an asymmetrical shawl.

FINISHED MEASUREMENTS
Width at wide end 13"/33cm
Width at narrow end 9"/23cm
Length of rectangle before seaming 45"/114cm

MATERIALS
- Two 3½oz/100g hanks (each approx 437yd/400m) of Cascade Yarns *Heritage Silk Paints* (superwash merino wool/mulberry silk) in #5673 lilac **1** Slight variations in color can occur with handpainted yarns, and can occur between dye lots.
- One pair each sizes 1, 2, 3, and 4 (2.25, 2.75, 3.25, and 3.5mm) needles *or size to obtain gauge*
- Stitch markers

GAUGE
25 sts and 36 rows to 4"/10cm over lace pat using size 3 (3.25mm) needles. *Take time to check gauge.*

LACE PATTERN (multiple of 6 sts)
Row 1 (RS) Knit.
Row 2 Purl.
Row 3 *K1, yo, p1, p2tog and return to LH needle, pass next st over the p2tog and return to RH needle, p1, yo; rep from * to end.
Row 4 Purl.
Rep rows 1–4 for lace pattern.

SHAWL
With size 1 (2.25mm) needles, cast on 86 sts. Knit 1 row, purl 1 row.

Begin lace pat
Row 1 (RS) K5 (garter st edge), yo, k2tog, k5, work row 1 of lace pat to last 8 sts, ssk, yo, k1, move yarn to front and sl last 5 sts purlwise (for I-cord edge).
Row 2 (WS) Pulling yarn tightly across WS, k5 (for I-cord edge), p3, work row 2 of lace pat to last 12 sts, p7, k5 (garter st edge).
Row 3 K5, yo, k2tog, yo, p1, p2tog and return to LH needle, pass next st over the p2tog and return to RH needle, p1, yo, work row 3 of lace pat to last 8 sts, ssk, yo, k1, move yarn to front and sl last 5 sts purlwise.
Row 4 Pulling yarn tightly across WS, k5, p3, work row 4 of lace pat to last 12 sts, p7, k5.
Cont to work lace pat in this manner until piece measures 5"/12.5cm from beg, end with a WS row. Change to size 2 (2.75mm) needles. Cont in lace pat until piece measures 10"/25.5cm from beg. Change to size 3 (3.25mm) needles. Cont in lace pat until piece measures 40"/101.5cm from beg. Change to size 4 (3.5mm) needles. Cont in lace pat until piece measures 45"/114cm from beg, end with a row 4.
Next row (RS) K to last 5 sts, sl 5 purlwise wyib.
Next row K5 for I-cord, p to last 5 sts, k5.
Knit 1 row. Bind off.

FINISHING
Block gently to measurements. Place a marker on the I-cord edge 9"/23cm up from bound-off edge. With RS facing, sew the cast-on edge under the I-cord from the marker to the bound-off edge. ∎

Florence

DESIGNED BY BARB BROWN

Color takes center stage in a Fair Isle cowl featuring a floral motif
overlayed with stripes and bordered by corrugated ribbing.

FINISHED MEASUREMENTS
Circumference 26"/66cm
Length 8¼"/21cm

MATERIALS
- One 3½oz/100g hank (each approx 437yd/400m) of
Cascade Yarns *Heritage* (superwash merino wool/
nylon) each in #5627 black (A), #5629 citron (B),
#5618 white (C), #5646 pumpkin (D), and #5642
blood orange (E) **①**
- Size 3 (3.25mm) circular needle, 24"/60cm long, *or
size to obtain gauge*
- Stitch marker

GAUGE
30 sts and 36 rnds to 4"/10cm over chart pat using
size 3 (3.25mm) needle.
Take time to check gauge.

COWL
With A, cast on 200 sts. Join, being careful not to
twist sts, and place marker for beg of rnds.
Knit 4 rnds.
Next rnd *K1 A, k1 B; rep from * around.
Next rnd *K1 A, p1 B; rep from * around for
corrugated rib.
Work 8 rnds more in corrugated rib. Break B.
Knit 4 rnds A, inc 8 sts evenly on last rnd.

Begin chart 1
Rnd 1 Work 16-st rep 13 times around.
Cont in this manner until rnd 13 of chart 1 is complete.
Knit 3 rnds A.

Begin chart 2
Rnd 1 Work 16-st rep 13 times around.
Cont in this manner until rnd 13 of chart 2
is complete.
Knit 3 rnds A.

Begin chart 3
Rnd 1 Work 16-st rep 13 times around.
Cont in this manner until rnd 14 of chart 3
is complete.
Knit 4 rnds A, dec 8 sts evenly on first rnd.

Next rnd *K1 A, k1 B; rep from * around.
Work 9 rnds corrugated rib as for beg. Break B. Knit 4
rnds A. Bind off.

FINISHING
Block if necessary, allowing edges to roll. ■

CHART 1

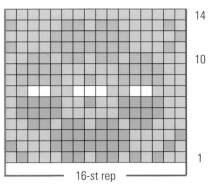

14
10
1

16-st rep

CHART 2

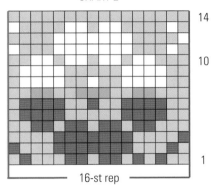

14
10
1

16-st rep

CHART 3

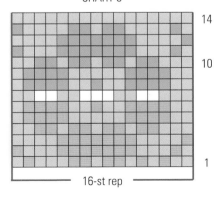

14
10
1

16-st rep

COLOR KEY

- A
- B
- C
- D
- E

Amelia

DESIGNED BY CHERYL MURRAY

An ombré effect elevates a chevron stitch scarf made in two halves and grafted.

FINISHED MEASUREMENTS
Approx 8 x 70"/20.5 x 178cm

MATERIALS
- One 3½oz/100g hank (each approx 437yd/400m) of Cascade Yarns *Heritage* (superwash merino wool/nylon) each in #5638 walnut (A), #5610 camel (B), and #5681 limestone (C)
- One pair size 7 (4.5mm) needles *or size to obtain gauge*
- Stitch markers
- 3"/7.5cm square of cardboard for tassels

GAUGE
22 sts and 28 rows to 4"/10cm over chevron pat using size 7 (4.5mm) needles with 2 strands held tog. *Take time to check gauge.*

CHEVRON PATTERN
(multiple of 14 sts plus 13)
Row 1 (WS) Purl. **Row 2** M1L, k5, S2KP, *K5, M1R, k1, M1L, k5, S2KP; rep from * to last 6 sts, K5, M1R.
Rep rows 1 and 2 for chevron pat.

NOTE
Scarf is worked in 2 halves with 2 strands held together. The halves are grafted to finish.

SCARF—FIRST HALF
With 2 strands of A held tog, cast on 47 sts.
Next row (WS) K3, place marker, p to last 3 sts, place marker, k3. **Next row** K3, work row 2 of chevron pat to marker, k3.
Cont in this manner, knitting first and last 3 sts of every row for a garter st edge and working chevron pat between markers until piece measures approx 14"/35.5cm from beg, end with a RS row. Break 1 strand of A. With 1 strand of A and 1 strand of B held tog, cont in pats as established until piece measures 28"/71cm from beg, end with a RS row. Break A.
Join a 2nd strand of B and cont in pats until piece measures 35"/89cm from beg, end with a RS row.

SECOND HALF
With 2 strands of C held tog, cast on 47 sts. Work in pats as for first half until piece measures approx 14"/35.5cm from beg, end with a RS row. Cut 1 strand of C. With 1 strand of C and 1 strand of B held tog, cont in pats as established until piece measures 28"/71cm from beg, end with a RS row. Cut C.
Join a 2nd strand of B and cont in pats until piece measures 35"/89cm from beg, end with a RS row.

FINISHING
With RS facing, graft halves using Kitchener st. Make 3 tassels each in A and C: Wrap yarn 50 times around 3"/7.5cm cardboard square. Insert 8"/20.5cm strand under top of wrapped strands and tie tightly, leaving tails. Cut lower edge of wrapped strands. Wrap 12"/30.5cm strand of yarn tightly around bundle, 1"/2.5cm below top. Pull ends to inside. Use tails to attach each tassel to one chevron point, matching colors. ∎

Susan

DESIGNED BY ANN MCDONALD KELLY

A paisley Fair Isle pattern is worked in the round,
then steeked to make the fringe on a stunning oversize scarf.

■■■■▶

FINISHED MEASUREMENTS
Approx 16½ x 64"/42 x 162.5cm excluding fringe

MATERIALS
- Two 3½oz/100g hanks (each approx 437yd/400m) of Cascade Yarns *Heritage* (superwash merino wool/nylon) each in #5612 moss (MC) and #5637 cerulean (CC) **(1)**
- Sizes 2 and 3 (2.75 and 3.25mm) circular needles, each 60"/150cm long, *or size to obtain gauge*
- Stitch markers

GAUGE
28 sts and 34 rnds to 4"/10cm over St st using larger needles.
Take time to check gauge.

STEEK PATTERN
Rnd 1 *K1 in MC, k1 in CC; rep from * to marker.
Rnd 2 *K1 in CC, k1 in MC; rep from * to marker.
Rep rnds 1 and 2 for steek pat.

NOTES
1) Shawl is worked in the round with a 60-st steek, which is cut and unraveled to make fringe.
2) Carry the color not in use loosely across the WS of work.

WRAP
With smaller needle and CC, cast on 505 sts. Join, being careful not to twist sts, and place marker (pm) for beg of rnd.
Next rnd K30, pm, k to last 30 sts, pm, k30.
Purl 1 rnd. Cont in garter st (k 1 rnd, p 1 rnd) for 4 rnds more. Change to larger needle and MC. Knit 2 rnds.

Begin charts
Rnd 1 Work steek pat to marker, sl marker, work 24-st rep of chart 1 for 18 times, rep sts 1–13, sl marker, work steek pat to end.
Cont to work chart 1 in this manner until rnd 18 is complete, then work chart 2 and chart 3 in the same way.
Work charts 1–3 once more, then work chart 1 once more—126 chart rnds complete. Knit 2 rnds in MC. Change to smaller needle and CC. Work 6 rnds in garter st. Bind off.

FINISHING
Cut steek between the first and last sts of rnd from cast-on edge to bound-off edge.

Fringe
Beg at cast-on edge, unravel steek sts to beg of chart pat. Make a knot with every 10 strands and snug tightly to end of shawl. ■

CHART 1

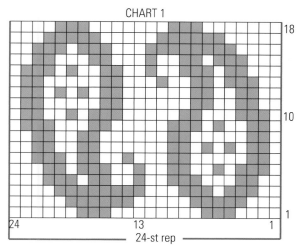

18

10

1

24   13   1

24-st rep

CHART 2

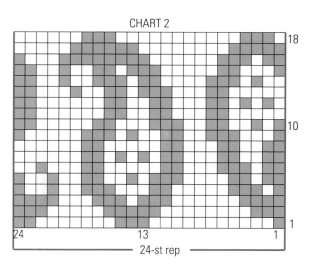

18

10

1

24   13   1

24-st rep

COLOR KEY

☐ MC

▨ CC

CHART 3

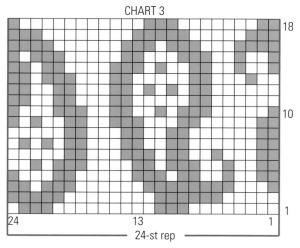

18

10

1

24   13   1

24-st rep

Nellie

DESIGNED BY ASHLEY RAO

A traditional Mayan motif is worked mosaic style, with four squares sewn together and finished with a picot edge and braided ties.

FINISHED MEASUREMENTS
Approx 17 x 17"/43 x 43cm

MATERIALS
- One 3½oz/100g hank (each approx 437yd/400m) of Cascade Yarns *Heritage* (superwash merino wool/nylon) each in #5618 snow (A), #5603 marine (B), and #5607 red (C) ①
- One pair size 2 (2.75mm) needles *or size to obtain gauge*
- Size 2 (2.75mm) circular needle, 24"/60cm long, for picot edge

GAUGE
27 sts and 56 rows to 4"/10cm over chart pat using size 2 (2.75mm) needles.
Take time to check gauge.

NOTES
1) Each row of the mosaic chart represents 2 worked rows. RS rows are read from right to left, WS rows are read from left to right.
2) The first st of each row indicates the color used to work the row. A rows are worked by knitting A sts and slipping B sts on the RS and purling A sts and slipping B sts on the WS; B rows are worked by knitting B sts and slipping A sts on both RS and WS rows.
3) Work shaping only on RS rows.
4) Slip the first st of every RS row knitwise; slip the first st of every WS row purlwise.

MOSAIC SQUARE (MAKE 4)
With B, cast on 3 sts.
Work chart through row 173. Bind off rem 3 sts knitwise on WS with B.

FINISHING
Sew upper edges of mosaic squares tog to form large square.

Picot edge
With RS facing, C, and circular needle, pick up 90 sts along each edge—360 sts.
Work picot bind-off as foll: *Cast on 2 sts, bind off 5 sts, return last st to LH needle; rep from * until all sts are bound off. Fasten off.

Ties
Cut 6 strands of C, each 24"/60cm long. Thread the 6 strands through one corner of bandana and adjust to even the ends. Holding 4 strands tog, braid ends for 6"/15cm and secure with a firm knot. Repeat for 2nd tie. ■

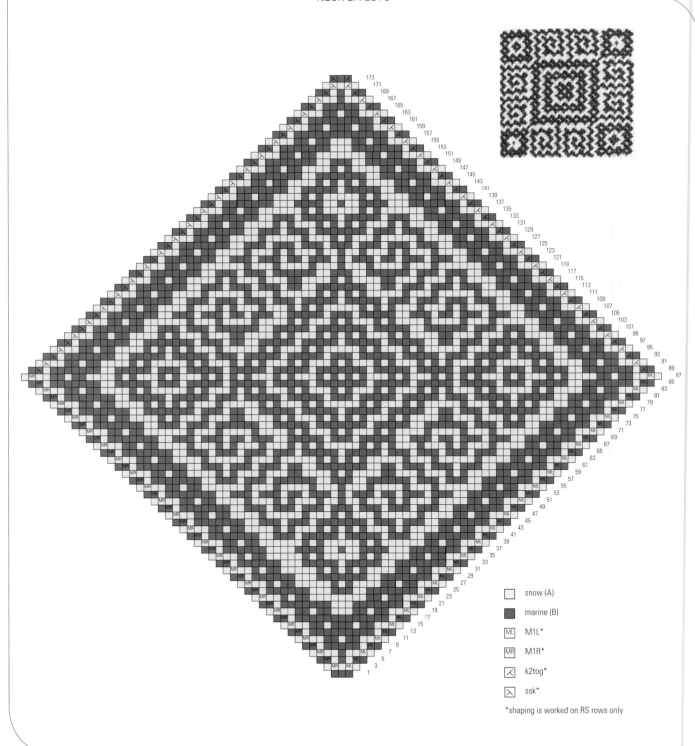

snow (A)

marine (B)

ML M1L*

MR M1R*

k2tog*

ssk*

*shaping is worked on RS rows only

Georgia

DESIGNED BY CHRISTINE COOK

A crescent-shaped shawlette is accented with columns of eyelets
and an oh-so-pretty ruffled lace border.

FINISHED MEASUREMENTS
Upper edge (from point to point) 29"/73.5cm
Length (at center) 9½"/24cm

MATERIALS
- One 3½oz/100g hank (each approx 437yd/400m) of
  Cascade Yarns *Heritage* (superwash merino wool/
  nylon) in #5617 raspberry (1)
- Size 5 (3.75mm) circular needle, 29"/74cm long, *or
  size to obtain gauge*
- Stitch markers

GAUGE
24 sts and 32 rows to 4"/10cm before blocking over
St st using size 5 (3.75mm) needles.
Take time to check gauge.

NOTES
1) Piece is worked from the neck to the border.
2) Piece is worked back and forth in rows. Circular
needle is used to accommodate large number of sts.
Do not join.

SHAWLETTE
Cast on 29 sts. Knit 1 (WS) row.
Set-up row (RS) K3, [yo, k1] twice, place marker (pm), [yo, k9, yo, k1, pm] twice, yo, k1, yo, k3—37 sts.
Next row K3, yo, p to last 3 sts, slipping markers, yo, k3—39 sts.

Begin pat
Row 1 (RS) K3, yo, [k to 1 st before next marker, yo, k1, sl marker, yo] 3 times, k to last 3 sts, yo, k3—8 sts inc'd.
Row 2 K3, yo, p to last 3 sts, yo, k3—2 sts inc'd.
Rep rows 1 and 2 for pat 22 times more—269 sts.
Remove markers when working last WS row.

Begin border
Row 1 (RS) K11, yo, [pm, k19, yo] 13 times across, k11—283 sts.
Row 2 and all WS rows through row 16 K2, p to last 2 sts, k2.
Row 3 K9, k2tog, yo, k1, yo, [sl marker, ssk, k15, k2tog, yo, k1, yo] 13 times across, ssk, k9.
Row 5 (inc) K8, k2tog, [yo, k1] 3 times, *sl marker, ssk, k13, k2tog, [yo, k1] 3 times; rep from * 12 times more, ssk, k8—297 sts.

Row 7 (inc) K7, k2tog, [k1, yo] 4 times, k2, *sl marker, ssk, k11, k2tog, [k1, yo] 4 times, k2; rep from * 12 times more, ssk, k7—325 sts.
Row 9 (inc) K6, k2tog, [k2, yo] 5 times, *sl marker, ssk, k9, k2tog, [k2, yo] 5 times; rep from * 12 times more, ssk, k6—367 sts.
Row 11 (inc) K5, k2tog, [yo, k3] 5 times, yo, *sl marker, ssk, k7, k2tog, [yo, k3] 5 times, yo; rep from * 12 times more, ssk, k5—423 sts.
Row 13 (inc) K4, k2tog, [k3, yo] 7 times, *sl marker, ssk, k5, k2tog, [k3, yo] 7 times; rep from * 12 times more, ssk, k4—493 sts.
Row 15 (inc) K3, k2tog, [yo, k4] 7 times, yo, *sl marker, ssk, k3, k2tog, [yo, k4] 7 times, yo; rep from * 12 times more, ssk, k3—577 sts.
Row 17 (inc) K2, k2tog, [yo, k4] 9 times; *sl marker, ssk, k1, k2tog, [yo, k4] 9 times; rep from * 12 times more, ssk, k2—675 sts.
Next row (WS) Knit.
Bind off as foll: *K2tog tbl, return st to LH needle; rep from * until all sts are bound off.

FINISHING
Block shawl, pinning to form crescent shape and allowing border to ruffle. ■

Dorothea

DESIGNED BY DEBBIE O'NEILL

The waves of classic shale lace are emphasized by alternating two variegated colors in a graceful scarf worked from side to side.

FINISHED MEASUREMENTS
Approx 10 x 65½"/25.5 x 166cm

MATERIALS
- One 3½oz/100g hank (each approx 437yd/400m) of Cascade Yarns *Heritage Silk Paints* (superwash merino wool/mulberry silk) each in #9995 violets (A) and #9958 vino (B)
  Slight variations in color can occur with handpainted yarns, and can occur between dye lots.
- Size 3 (3.25mm) circular needle, 47"/120cm long, *or size to obtain gauge*

GAUGE
22 sts and 32 rows to 4"/10cm over old shale lace using size 3 (3.25mm) needle, after blocking.
Take time to check gauge.

OLD SHALE LACE
(multiple of 18 sts)
Row 1 (RS) Knit.
Row 2 Purl.
Row 3 *[K2tog] 3 times, [yo, k1] 6 times, [k2tog] 3 times; rep from * to end.
Row 4 Knit.
Rep rows 1–4 for old shale lace.

NOTES
1) Cast on and bind off loosely.

2) Scarf is worked back and forth in rows. Circular needle is used to accommodate large number of sts.
3) Carry color not in use up the side as you work.

SCARF
With A, cast on 360 sts loosely. Knit 4 rows.

Begin old shale lace
[Rep rows 1–4 of old shale lace twice; with B, rep rows 1–4 of old shale lace once] 5 times.
With A, rep rows 1–4 of old shale lace twice more.
Knit 3 rows. Bind off loosely.

FINISHING
Block scarf to size, allowing edges to scallop. ■

Abigail

DESIGNED BY FAINA GOBERSTEIN

Moss stitch alternates with two openwork patterns for a delicate, textured look,
while single crochet adds a polished finish to the sides.

FINISHED MEASUREMENTS
Approx 8 x 60"/20.5 x 152.5cm

MATERIALS
- Two 3½oz/100g hanks (each approx 437yd/400m) of Cascade Yarns *Heritage Silk* (superwash merino wool/mulberry silk) in #5681
- One pair size 4 (3.5mm) needles *or size to obtain gauge*
- Size G/6 (4mm) crochet hook

GAUGE
30 sts and 24 rows to 4"/10cm over double moss st using size 4 (3.5mm) needles.
Take time to check gauge.

DOUBLE MOSS STITCH
(multiple of 4 sts)
Row 1 (RS) *K2, p2; rep from * to end.
Row 2 K the knit sts and p the purl sts.
Row 3 *P2, k2; rep from * to end.
Row 4 K the knit sts and p the purl sts.
Rep rows 1–4 for double moss st.

PATTERN STITCH 1
(multiple of 4 sts)
Row 1 (RS) Knit.
Row 2 Knit.
Row 3 *K1, [yo] 3 times; rep from * to end.
Row 4 *[Drop 3 yos, sl 1] 4 times, return last 4 sts to LH needle, [k4tog tbl, p4tog tbl] twice in same st; rep from * to end.
Rows 5 and 6 Knit.
Work rows 1–6 for pat st 1.

PATTERN STITCH 2
Row 1 (RS) Knit.
Row 2 Knit.
Row 3 *K1, [yo] 3 times; rep from * to end.
Row 4 *[Wyif, drop 3 yos, sl 1] 4 times, bring yarn to back, return last 4 sts to LH needle, bring yarn to front, return same 4 sts to RH needle; rep from * to end.
Rows 5 and 6 Knit.
Work rows 1–6 for pat st 2.

NOTE
For selvedge edges, slip the first st of every row wyif and knit the last st of every row throughout.

SCARF
Cast on 58 sts.
*Row 1 (RS)** Sl 1 wyif, work in double moss st to last st, k1.

Row 2 Sl 1 wyif, work in double moss st to last st, k1. Cont to foll pat in this manner until row 4 is complete, rep rows 1 and 2.

Cont to sl the first st and k the last st of every row, work rows 1–6 of pat st 1.

Work 6 rows in double moss st. Work 6 rows in pat st 2. Rep from * 14 times more. Work 6 rows in double moss st. Work 6 rows of pat st 1. Work 6 rows in double moss st. Bind off loosely in pat.

FINISHING

Block to measurements. With crochet hook and RS facing, work 1 row of single crochet (sc) loosely along each side edge of scarf, working 1 sc in each selvedge st and 4 sc in each elongated selvedge st. Block edges. ■

Cleopatra

DESIGNED BY AMANDA BLAIR BROWN

Take two tones and give them a twist, in a scarf made from
two strips twisted in the center and joined to side strips.

FINISHED MEASUREMENTS
Approx 5 x 58"/12.5 x 147cm

MATERIALS
- One 3½oz/100g hank (each approx 437yd/400m) of
  Cascade Yarns *Heritage* (superwash merino wool/
  nylon) each in #5601 real black (A) and #5602 grey
  (B) ❶
- One set (5) size 3 (3.25mm) double-pointed needles
  (dpns) *or size to obtain gauge*
- Stitch holders

GAUGE
46 sts and 36 rows to 4"/10cm over k1, p1 rib using
size 3 (3.25mm) needles.
Take time to check gauge.

K1, P1 RIB
(over any number of sts)
Row 1 (RS) *K1, p1; rep from * to end.
Row 2 K the knit sts and p the purl sts.
Rep row 2 for k1, p1 rib.

NOTES
1) Piece is worked in 4 strips. The center 2 strips (1
and 3) are twisted around each other and knit to the
outer strips (2 and 4) as the piece is worked.
2) The inside stitch of each outer strip is dropped
when knitting is complete.
3) Piece is worked in rows. Double-pointed needles

are used to accommodate the small number of sts in each strip.

SCARF

With A and 2 dpns, cast on 29 sts.
Next row (RS) Work k1, p1 rib over 14 sts for strip 1, place rem 15 sts on st holder for strip 2.
Cont on strip 1, work in rib for 31 rows more. Set aside.
With B and 2 dpns, cast on 29 sts.
Next row (WS) Work k1, p1 rib over 14 sts for strip 3, place rem sts on st holder for strip 4.
Cont on strip 3, work in rib for 31 rows more. Set aside.

Begin pattern

**Lay strips 1 and 3 side by side and, keeping strips flat, take strip 1 behind and over strip 3.
Next (joining) row (RS) Work in rib over 14 strip 1 sts, then over 15 strip 2 sts.
Cont on strips 1 and 2, work in rib for 6 rows more.
Next row (WS) Work in rib over 14 strip 2 sts and place 15 sts for strip 1 on st holder.
Cont on strip 2, work in rib for 9 rows more.
Place strip 1 sts on needle and work in rib over 29 sts for strips 1 and 2 for 7 rows.
Next row (RS) Work in rib over 14 strip 1 sts, place 15 strip 2 sts on st holder.
Work 19 rows more on strip 1 and set aside.
Lay strips 1 and 3 side by side and, keeping strips flat, take strip 3 over and behind strip 1.
Next (joining) row (WS) Work in rib over 14 strip 3 sts, then over 15 strip 4 sts.
Cont on strips 3 and 4, work in rib for 6 rows more.
Next row (RS) Work in rib over 14 strip 4 sts and place 15 sts for strip 3 on st holder.

Cont on strip 4, work in rib for 9 rows more.
Place strip 3 sts on needle and work in rib for 29 sts for strips 3 and 4 for 7 rows.
Next row (WS) Work in rib over 14 strip 3 sts, place 15 strip 4 sts on st holder.
Work 19 rows more on strip 4 and set aside.
Rep from ** 19 times more or until desired length of scarf.

FINISHING

Work 10 rows more each on strip 1 and strip 3. Bind off strips 1 and 3. Bind off strips 2 and 4, dropping the inside st on each strip and letting it unravel to the lower edge of the scarf.
Sew strips 1 and 2 tog at lower edge of scarf. Sew strips 3 and 4 tog at lower edge of scarf.
Bringing strip 1 over strip 3, sew strip 1 to strip 2 at top edge of scarf. Sew strips 3 and 4 tog at top of scarf. ■

Gertrude

DESIGNED BY ANNA DAVIS

Small-scale chevron stripes and dainty buttons add sweet and subtle design flair to a simply shaped cowl.

FINISHED MEASUREMENTS
Approx 24 x 9½"/61 x 24cm

MATERIALS
- One 3½oz/100g hank (each approx 437yd/400m) of Cascade Yarns *Heritage* (superwash merino wool/nylon) each in #5627 jade (A), #5630 anis (B), and #5653 blue horizon (C) ❶
- Size 4 (3.5mm) circular needle, 32"/80cm long, *or size to obtain gauge*
- Five 7/16" (11mm) buttons
- Stitch markers

GAUGE
27 sts and 48 rows to 4"/10cm over chevron pat using size 4 (3.5mm) needles.
Take time to check gauge.

CHEVRON PATTERN
(multiple of 4 sts plus 1)
Row 1 (RS) K1, *sl 3, k1; rep from * to end.
Row 2 P2, *sl 1, p3; rep from * to last 3 sts, sl 1, p2.
Row 3 Knit.
Row 4 Purl.
Rep rows 1–4 for chevron pat.

STRIPE SEQUENCE
Work one 4-row rep in each color as foll: B, C, A, B, A, C; rep these 24 rows for stripe sequence.

SEED STITCH
(over an odd number of sts)
Row 1 (RS) *K1, p1; rep from * to last st, k1.
Row 2 K the purl sts and p the knit sts as they appear.
Rep row 2 for seed st.

NOTES
1) Cowl is worked in rows. Circular needle is used to accommodate large number of sts. Do not join.
2) Slip sts purlwise with yarn at WS of work.
3) Cowl is worked with St st selvedge sts throughout.

COWL
With A, cast on 147 sts. Do not join.
Next row (RS) K1 (selvedge), work in seed st to last st, k1 (selvedge).
Next row P1 (selvedge), work in seed st to last st, p1 (selvedge).
Cont in this way, work 4 rows more in seed st.

Begin chevron pat and stripe sequence
Keeping St st selvedge sts each side as established, beg chevron pat, changing color foll stripe sequence for every 4-row rep. Cont in this manner until piece measures 8¾"/22cm from beg, end with a row 4 in B. With A, work 6 rows in seed st. Bind off in pat.

FINISHING
Button band
With RS facing and A, beg at upper edge, pick up and k 59 sts evenly along side edge.

Next row (WS) *P1, k1; rep from * to last st, p1. Work 6 rows more in seed st as established. Bind off in pat.

Place markers for 5 buttons, with the first 1"/2.5cm from upper edge, the last 1"/2.5cm from lower edge, and the rest evenly spaced between.

Buttonhole band
With RS facing and A, beg at lower edge, pick up and k 59 sts evenly along side edge. Work 3 rows in seed st as for button band. In 4th row, work p2tog, yo for buttonholes to correspond to markers. Work 3 rows more, bind off in pat.

Block gently, if necessary. Sew on buttons. ■

Frida

DESIGNED BY CANDACE EISNER STRICK

Scallops in boldly contrasting colors make a statement border
on a garter stitch shawl with short row shaping.

FINISHED MEASUREMENTS
Wingspan after blocking 48"/122cm
Depth 12"/30.5cm

MATERIALS
- One 3½oz/100g hank (each approx 437yd/399.5m) of Cascade Yarns *Heritage Paints* (superwash merino wool/nylon) each in #9783 solar (A) and #9828 featherstone (B)
  Slight variations in color can occur with handpainted yarns, and can occur between dye lots.
- Size 3 (3.25mm) circular needle, 24"/60cm long, *or size to obtain gauge*
- Stitch markers
- Safety pins

GAUGE
24 sts and 52 rows to 4"/10cm over garter st using size 3 (3.25mm) needles.
Take time to check gauge.

STITCH GLOSSARY
CE (chain edge) Sl 1 purlwise wyif, move yarn to back between needles to work the next st.

NOTE
First tier of scallops is worked separately, then 2nd tier of scallops is picked up along edges of first tier. Garter st body is worked from completed 2nd tier of scallops.

SHAWL
Free scallops (make 7)
With A, cast on 47 sts.
Row 1 (WS) CE, knit to end.
Row 2 CE, k1, ssk, yo, k to last 4 sts, yo, k2tog, k2.
Row 3 (dec) CE, [k10, k2tog] 3 times, k10—44 sts.
Row 4 (inc) CE, k2, [yo, k2tog] 19 times, yo, k3—45 sts.
Row 5 (dec) CE, k4, [p2, k2] 9 times, k2tog, k2—44 sts.
Row 6 (dec) CE, k1, ssk, yo, ssk, k the k sts and p the purl sts for established rib to the last 6 sts, k2tog, yo, k2tog, k2—2 sts dec'd.
Row 7 CE, k2, p2, work in rib as established to the last 5 sts, p2, k3.
Rep rows 6 and 7 for 16 times more—10 sts.

Shape top

Next (dec) row (RS) CE, ssk, k2tog, k to end—
2 sts dec'd.

Next row CE, knit to end.

Rep last 2 rows twice more—4 sts.

Next row (RS) Sl 2 sts tog knitwise, k2tog, pass
the sl sts over the k2tog. Place rem st on safety pin.
Break yarn, leaving a 5"/12.5cm tail.

JOINING FREE SCALLOPS

Scallop 8

With B, cast on 24 sts, with RS facing and beg at
cast-on edge, pick up and k 23 sts along the RH edge
of first free scallop—47 sts.

Row 1 (dec WS) CE, [k10, k2tog] 3 times, k10—44 sts.

Row 2 (inc) CE, k2, [yo, k2tog] 19 times, yo, k3—
45 sts.

Row 3 (dec) CE, k4, [p2, k2] 9 times, k2tog, k2—
44 sts.

Begin short rows

Short row 1 (RS) CE, k2, rib 20 sts, turn.

Short row 2 Yo, rib 2 sts, turn.

Short row 3 Yo, rib to yo in previous row, work yo
tog in pat with next st, turn.

Rep short row 3 until 4 sts rem after the yos on
each side.

Next row (RS) Yo, rib to yo in previous row, work yo
tog in pat with next st, k3.

Next row (WS) CE, rib to yo in previous row, work
yo tog in pat with next st, k to end, turn.

Keep sts on RH needle while working rem scallops.

Scallops 9, 10, 11, 12, 13, and 14

With B and RS facing, beg below stitch on pin, pick
up and k 23 sts along LH side of scallop just joined,
cast on 1 st, beg at cast-on edge, pick up and k 23 sts
along RH edge of next free scallop—47 sts.
Complete as for scallop 8.

Scallop 15

With B and RS facing, beg below stitch on pin, pick
up and k 23 sts along LH side of scallop just joined,
cast on 24 sts. Complete as for scallop 8. Break B.

Shawl body

With RS facing and A, [pick up and k 2 sts in CE along
edge of scallop, k44, pick up and k 2 sts in CE along
edge of scallop, k st from pin] 7 times, pick up and k 2
sts in CE along edge of last scallop, k to end, pick up
and k 2 sts in CE along edge of last scallop—391 sts.
Knit 1 row.

Next (eyelet) row (RS) K2, *yo, k2tog; rep from *
to last st, k1.

Next (inc) row K3, kfb, k to end—392 sts. Break A.

Begin short rows

Next (short) row (RS) With B, k191, place marker
(pm), k10, pm, turn.

Next (short) row K to 1 st before marker, remove
marker, k2tog, k3, pm, turn.

Next (short) row (RS) K to 1 st before marker,
remove marker, ssk, k3, pm, turn.

Rep last 2 short rows until 2 sts rem after the
decrease, end with a RS row—296 sts.

Next row (WS) Knit. Break yarn.

With A, knit 1 row and dec 36 sts evenly spaced
across—260 sts.

Next (eyelet) row (WS) P2, *yo, p2tog; rep from *
to last 2 sts, p2.

Knit 2 rows.

Bind off as foll: *K2tog tbl, return st to LH needle; rep
from * until all sts are bound off. Fasten off last st.

Block to measurements. ■

Helen

DESIGNED BY TABETHA HEDRICK

A long cowl that features an offset ribbed cable pattern works up quickly
with two strands of yarn held together.

FINISHED MEASUREMENTS
Circumference 62"/157.5cm
Width 4"/10cm

MATERIALS
- Two 3½oz/100g hanks (each approx 437yd/400m) of Cascade Yarns *Heritage Silk* (superwash merino wool/mulberry silk) in #5617 raspberry (1)
- One pair size 7 (4.5mm) needles *or size to obtain gauge*
- Spare needle for 3-needle bind-off
- Size 7 (4.5mm) crochet hook for provisional cast-on
- Cable needle (cn)
- Scrap yarn

GAUGE
40 sts and 23 rows to 4"/10cm over pat st using size 7 (4.5mm) needles and 2 strands of yarn held tog.
Take time to check gauge.

STITCH GLOSSARY
6-st RRC (6-st right ribbed cable) Sl 5 sts to cn and hold to *back*, k1; k1, p2, k2 from cn.

PROVISIONAL CAST-ON
Using scrap yarn and crochet hook, chain the number of sts to cast on, plus a few extra. Cut a tail and pull the tail through the last chain. With knitting needle and yarn, pick up and knit the stated number of sts through the "purl bumps" on the back of the chain. To remove scrap chain, when instructed, pull out the tail from the last crochet st. Gently and slowly pull on the tail to unravel the crochet sts, carefully placing each released knit st on a needle.

3-NEEDLE BIND-OFF
1) Hold right sides of pieces together on 2 needles. Insert 3rd needle into first st of each needle and wrap yarn knitwise.
2) Knit these 2 sts together and slip them off the needles to the RH needle. *Knit the next 2 sts together in the same manner.
3) Pass first st on RH needle over 2nd st on RH needle. Rep from * in step 2 until all sts have been bound off and 1 st rem on RH needle. Break yarn and fasten off.

PATTERN STITCH
(multiple of 8 sts plus 6, plus 2 selvedge sts)
Row 1 (RS) Sl 1 (selvedge), *6-st RRC, p2; rep from * to last 7 sts, 6-st RRC, k1.
Row 2 Sl 1 (selvedge), *p2, k2; rep from * to last 3 sts, p3.
Row 3 Sl 1, *k2, p2; rep from * to last 3 sts, k3.
Rows 4–6 Rep rows 2 and 3 once more, then row 2 once.
Row 7 Sl 1, k2, *p2, 6-st RRC; rep from * to last 5 sts, p2, k3.
Rows 8–12 Rep rows 2–6.
Rep rows 1–12 for pat st.

NOTES

1) Slip selvedge sts (first st of each row) with yarn at WS of work.

2) Cowl is worked with 2 strands of yarn held tog throughout.

COWL

With 2 strands of yarn held tog, cast on 40 sts using provisional cast-on method.

Set-up row (WS) Sl 1, *p2, k2; rep from * to last 3 sts, p3.

Begin pattern st

Rep rows 1–12 of pat st until piece measures approx 62"/157.5cm from beg.

FINISHING

Carefully remove scrap yarn and place sts on a needle. With spare needle, join ends using 3-needle bind-off method.

Block to maximum size. Rib will draw in after the cowl is dry and has been unpinned. ∎

Eleanor

DESIGNED BY JACQUELINE VAN DILLEN

Panels of ribbing and moss stitch form a uniquely shaped neckwarmer
with a jaunty foldover buttoned collar.

FINISHED MEASUREMENTS
Approximately 8 x 42"/12.5 x 106.5cm

MATERIALS
• One 3½oz/100g hank (each approx 437yd/400m)
  of Cascade Yarns *Heritage Silk Paints* (superwash
  merino wool/nylon) in #9788 winter (**1**)
  Slight variations in color can occur with
  handpainted yarns, and can occur between dye
  lots.
• One pair size 3 (3mm) needles *or size to
  obtain gauge*
• Three ⅞" (22mm) buttons
• Stitch markers

GAUGE
28 sts and 36 rows to 4"/10cm over moss st using
size 3 (3mm) needles. *Take time to check gauge.*

K1, P1 RIB
(over an even number of sts)
Row 1 (RS) *K1, p1; rep from * to end.
Row 2 K the knit sts and p the purl sts as
they appear.
Rep row 2 for k1, p1 rib.

MOSS STITCH

(over an even number of sts)
Row 1 (RS) *K1, p1; rep from * to end.
Row 2 K the knit sts and p the purl sts as they appear.
Row 3 *P1, k1; rep from * to end.
Row 4 K the knit sts and p the purl sts as they appear.
Rep rows 1–4 for moss st.

NECKWARMER

Cast on 2 sts.
Row 1 (RS) K2.
Row 2 P1, M1, p1—3 sts.
Row 3 Sl 1, k2.
Row 4 Sl 1, M1, p2—4 sts.
Row 5 Sl 1, k1, p1, k1.
Row 6 (inc) Sl 1, M1, k1, p2—5 sts.
Row 7 Sl 1, [k1, p1] twice.
Row 8 Sl 1, M1, work in rib as established to last 2 sts, p2—1 st inc'd.
Row 9 Sl 1, work in rib as established.
Row 10 Sl 1, M1, work in rib as established to last 2 sts, p2—1 st inc'd.
Rep last 2 rows 14 times more, slipping first st of every row and working incs into k1, p1 rib—20 sts.

Begin moss st

Next row (RS) Sl 1, rib 9 sts, place marker, yo, place marker, rib to end—21 sts.

Next row Sl 1, rib to marker, sl marker, p1, sl marker, rib to end.
Next row Sl 1, rib to marker, sl marker, k1, yo, sl marker, rib to end—1 st inc'd.
Next row Sl 1, rib to marker, sl marker, work in moss st to next marker, yo, sl marker, rib to end.
Cont in this manner, working sts outside of markers in rib as established, and center sts in moss st and working inc'd sts into moss st. Rep inc row every other row 42 times more—64 sts.
Work even until piece measures 16"/40.5cm from beg. Work in rib pat as established over all sts until piece measures 41"/104cm from beg, end with a WS row.
Next (buttonhole) row (RS) Rib 6 sts, [bind off 4 sts, rib until there are 20 sts on RH needle after last buttonhole] twice, bind off 4 sts, rib to end.
Next row Work in rib, casting on 4 sts over each buttonhole.
Rib 3 rows more. Bind off in pat.

FINISHING

Sew 1 button to RS of rib on shaped side of scarf, approx 16"/40.5cm from pointed beg of scarf. Button first button with RS of buttonhole facing. Place markers for 2 more buttons to correspond to rem buttonholes. To wear, button first button through first buttonhole, then fold edge of scarf over to button center button through 2 rem buttonholes. See photo. ■

Betsy

DESIGNED BY PAT OLSKI

Beautifully intricate lace motifs adorn the back and extensions of a stole
with a unique shape and keyhole closure.

FINISHED MEASUREMENTS
Width of back 16"/41cm
Length to back neck 9"/23cm
Length from back neck to front point 33"/84cm

MATERIALS
- One 3½oz/100g hank (each approx 437yd/400m) of Cascade Yarns *Heritage Silk* (superwash merino wool/mulberry silk) in #5660 grey
- One pair size 7 (4.5mm) needles *or size to obtain gauge*
- Stitch markers

GAUGE
21 sts and 24 rows to 4"/10cm over St st using size 7 (4.5mm) needles. *Take time to check gauge.*

NOTE
Piece is worked from lower edge of back to the points of the front.

STITCH GLOSSARY
MB (make bobble) Knit into front, back, front, back, and front of st—5 sts inc. Pass 1st–4th sts over 5th st.

STOLE
Cast on 82 sts. Knit 10 rows. Place markers 5 sts from each edge for garter st edges.
Next row (RS) K5, sl marker, k1, k2tog, k1 yo, k1tbl, [yo, k1, ssk, k2tog, k1, yo, k1tbl] 9 times, yo, k1, k2tog, k1, sl marker, k5.
Next row K5, sl marker, p to next marker, sl marker, k5.
Rep last 2 rows 4 times more.
Keeping first and last 5 sts in garter st, work 2 rows in St st, inc 1 st in center of last row—83 sts.

Begin charts 1 and 2
Row 1 (RS) K to marker, sl marker, work chart 1 over 37 sts, work chart 2 over 36 sts, sl marker, k to end.
Row 2 K to marker, sl marker, work chart 2 over 36 sts, work chart 1 over 37 sts, sl marker, k to end.
Cont to work charts in this manner until row 24 is complete.

Begin charts 3 and 4
Row 1 (RS) K to marker, sl marker, work chart 3 over 37 sts, work chart 4 over 36 sts, sl marker, k to end.
Row 2 K to marker, sl marker, work chart 4 over 36 sts, work chart 3 over 37 sts, sl marker, k to end.
Cont to work charts in this manner until row 24 is complete.

Shape neck and begin chart 5

Row 1 K to marker, sl marker, work chart 5 over 21 sts, pm, k9, join a 2nd ball of yarn and bind off next 13 sts, k9, pm, work chart 5 over 21 sts, sl marker, k to end.

Cont on the sts for the left side only, work in garter st outside of markers and cont in chart pat as established until row 12 is complete, AT THE SAME TIME, shape neck as foll:

Bind off 2 sts at beg of next RS row, then dec 1 st at neck edge every other row twice—31 sts for left side.

Keeping first and last 5 sts each side in garter st, rep rows 1–12 of chart 5 for 14 times more, end with a row 12.

Begin chart 6

Next row (RS) Work chart 6 over 31 sts.

Cont to work chart until row 26 is complete. Bind off rem 7 sts.

Right side

With WS facing, rejoin yarn to cont to work right side.

Next row (WS) Bind off 2 sts, k to marker, sl marker, work row 2 of chart 5 over 21 sts, sl marker, k5. Cont as for left side until chart row 12 has been worked 7 times total, rep rows 1 and 2.

Keyhole

Row 1 (RS) K to marker, sl marker, k4, ssk, yo, k3, ssk; join 2nd ball of yarn, k4, yo, ssk, k to end.

Row 2 K to marker, sl marker, p7, k3; with 2nd ball of yarn, k3, p7, k to end.

Row 3 (RS) K to marker, sl marker, k3, ssk, yo, k4, sl 1 wyif; with 2nd ball of yarn, k5, yo, k2tog, k to end.

Row 4 Rep row 2.

Row 5 K to marker, sl marker, k2, k2tog, yo, k to last st, sl 1 wyif; with 2nd ball of yarn, k6, yo, k2tog, k to end.

Row 6 Rep row 2.

Rep rows 5 and 6 for 10 times more.

CHART 1

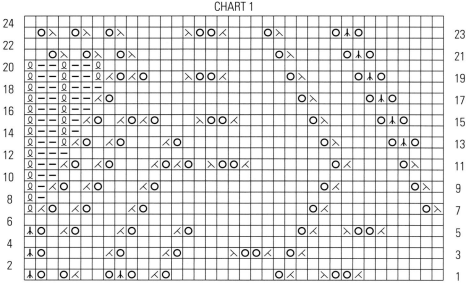

37 sts

CHART 2

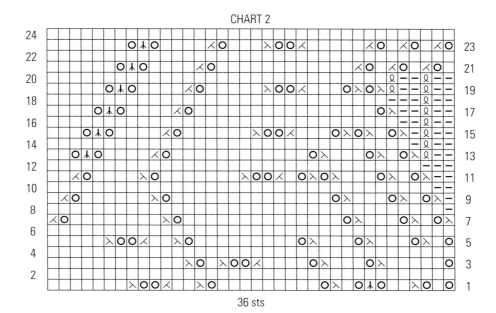

36 sts

CHART 3

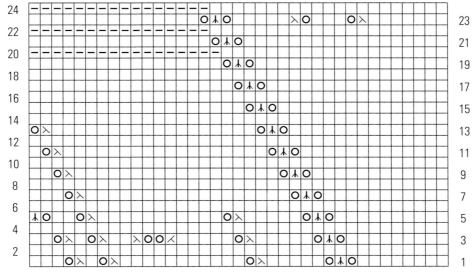

37 sts

CHART 4

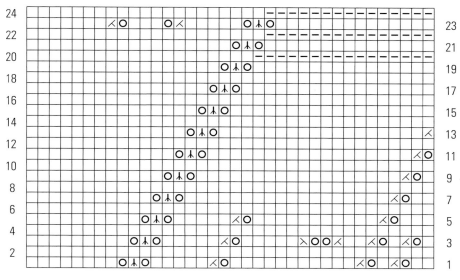

36 sts

CHART 5

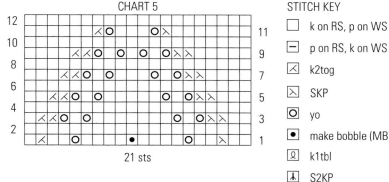

21 sts

STITCH KEY

☐	k on RS, p on WS
▬	p on RS, k on WS
◿	k2tog
◺	SKP
◉	yo
●	make bobble (MB)
☖	k1tbl
⟱	S2KP

Next 2 rows Rep rows 3 and 4.
Next row (RS) K to marker, sl marker, k4, ssk, yo, k4, M1, k4, yo, k2tog, k to end.
Next row K to marker, sl marker, p7, k7, p to marker, sl marker, k to end.
Next row Knit.
Next row K to marker, sl marker, p7, k7, p to marker, sl marker, k to end.
Rep last 2 rows once more.

Begin chart 5
Keeping first and last 5 sts in garter st rep rows 1–12 of chart 5 for 5 times.

Begin chart 6
Next row (RS) Work chart 6 over 31 sts.
Cont to work chart until row 26 is complete. Bind off rem 7 sts. ■

CHART 6

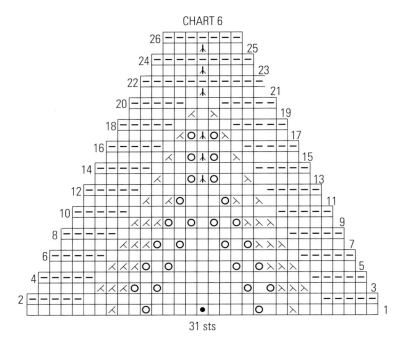

31 sts

STITCH KEY

☐	k on RS, p on WS
⊟	p on RS, k on WS
◹	k2tog
◺	SKP
⊙	yo
⊡	make bobble (MB)
⍭	k1tbl
⍓	S2KP

Louisa

DESIGNED BY CYNTHIA YANOK

Two patterns are better than one: two-color slip stitch meets a simple lace motif halfway, with seed stitch edges tying them together.

FINISHED MEASUREMENTS
Circumference 42½"/108cm
Width 9¾"/24.5cm

MATERIALS
- One 3½oz/100g hank (each approx 437yd/400m) of Cascade Yarns *Heritage* (superwash merino wool/nylon) each in #5660 grey (A) and #5611 butter (B) ⬤
- One pair size 3 (3.25mm) needles *or size to obtain gauge*
- Size E/4 (3.5mm) crochet hook and scrap yarn for provisional cast-on
- Stitch markers

GAUGE
26 sts and 36 rows to 4"/10cm after blocking over St st using size 3 (3.25mm) needles.
Take time to check gauge.

PROVISIONAL CAST-ON
Using scrap yarn and crochet hook, chain the number of sts to cast on, plus a few extra. Cut a tail and pull the tail through the last chain. With knitting needle and yarn, pick up and knit the stated number of sts through the "purl bumps" on the back of the chain. To remove scrap chain, when instructed, pull out the tail from the last crochet st. Gently and slowly pull on the tail to unravel the crochet sts, carefully placing each released knit st on a needle.

SEED STITCH
(over an odd number of sts)
Row 1 *K1, p1; rep from * to last st, k1.
Row 2 K the purl sts and p the knit sts as they appear.
Rep row 2 for seed st.

LACE PATTERN

(over an even number of sts)

Note that pattern has 7 rows, so the RS and WS will be reversed for each 7-row rep.

Row 1 K1, *yo, k1; rep from * to last st, k1.

Row 2 K1, p to last st, k1.

Row 3 K1, *k2tog; rep from * to last st, k1.

Rows 4 and 5 K1, *yo, k2tog; rep from * to last st, k1.

Rows 6 and 7 Knit.

Rep rows 1–7 for lace pat.

NOTES

1) Twist yarns on WS when changing colors to prevent holes.

2) Slip sts purlwise with yarn in back on RS rows and with yarn in front on WS rows.

3) The first and last sts of every row are worked in seed st.

COWL

With A, cast on 73 sts using provisional cast-on method.

Set-up row (RS) K3, place marker (pm), k to last 3 sts, pm, k to end.

Row 1 (WS) With A, work in seed st to marker, sl marker, purl to marker, sl marker, work in seed st to end.

Row 2 With A, work in seed st to marker, sl marker, with B, k3, *sl 1, k3; rep from * to marker, sl marker, work in seed st to end.

Row 3 With B, work to marker, sl marker, p3, *sl 1, p3; rep from * to marker, sl marker, with A, work to end.

Row 4 With A, work to marker, sl marker, with B, k3, *sl 1, k3; rep from * to marker, sl marker, work to end.

Row 5 With B, work to marker, sl marker, purl to marker, sl marker, work to end.

Row 6 With B, work to marker, sl marker, with A, k3, *sl 1, k3; rep from * to marker, sl marker, work to end.

Row 7 With A, work to marker, sl marker, p3, *sl 1, p3; rep from * to marker, sl marker, with B, work to end.

Row 8 With B, work to marker, sl marker, with A, k3, *sl 1, k3; rep from * to marker, sl marker, work to end.

Rep rows 1–8 for sl st pat with seed st edges, until piece measures approx 21"/53.5cm from beg, end with a row 8. Break B.

Next (dec) row (WS) With A, work to marker, sl marker, *[p2tog] twice, p1; rep from * to 2 sts before marker, p2tog, sl marker, work to end—46 sts.

Begin lace pat

With A only, cont to work 3 sts in seed st at beg and end of every row as established, rep rows 1–7 of lace pat until piece measures approx 42"/106.5cm from beg, end with a row 7. Break yarn, leaving a tail approx 48"/122cm long. Carefully remove scrap yarn from provisional cast-on and place sts on a needle. With RS facing, graft ends tog. ■

Simone

DESIGNED BY DEBBIE O'NEILL

A pretty repeating eyelet ridge detail lifts a stockinette
stitch triangle shawl into another design dimension.

FINISHED MEASUREMENTS
Width across upper edge 64"/162.5cm
Length from neck to point 22½"/57cm

MATERIALS
• Two 3½oz/100g hanks (each approx 437yd/399.5m)
  of Cascade Yarns *Heritage Paints* (superwash
  merino wool/nylon) 🔢
  Note: The color pictured has been discontinued.
  As an alternative, we suggest #9780 fjord.
• Size 3 (3.25mm) circular needle, 47"/120cm long, *or
  size to obtain gauge*
• Stitch markers

GAUGE
32 sts and 36 rows to 4"/10cm over St st using size 3
(3.25mm) needles.
Take time to check gauge.

EYELET RIDGE
Rows 1, 3, and 7 (RS) K2, [sl marker, yo, k to marker,
yo, sl marker, k2] twice.
Rows 2, 4, and 6 Knit, slipping markers.
Row 5 K2, sl marker, [yo, *k2tog, yo; rep from *
to 1 st, before marker, sl marker, k1 yo, sl marker,
k2] twice.
Row 8 Knit.
Work rows 1–8 for an eyelet ridge.

NOTE
Shawl is worked in back and forth in rows. Circular
needle is used to accommodate large number of sts.
Do not join.

SHAWL

Cast on 8 sts.

Next (set-up) row (WS) K2, [place marker (pm), k1, pm, k2] twice.

Next (inc) row (RS) K2, [sl marker, yo, k to marker, yo, sl marker, k2] twice—4 sts inc'd.

Next row Knit.

Rep last 2 rows once more—16 sts.

Begin pattern

Row 1 (RS) K2, [sl marker, yo, k to marker, yo, sl marker, k2] twice—4 sts inc'd.

Row 2 Purl.

Rep rows 1 and 2 for pat st 10 times more—60 sts.

Work one eyelet ridge—76 sts.

Work 12 rows in pat st—100 sts.

Work one eyelet ridge—116 sts.

Work 24 rows in pat st—164 sts.

Work one eyelet ridge—180 sts.

Work 14 rows in pat st—208 sts.

Work one eyelet ridge—224 sts.

Work 28 rows in pat st—280 sts.

Work one eyelet ridge—296 sts.

Work 8 rows in pat st—312 sts.

Work one eyelet ridge—328 sts.

Work 1 row in pat st—332 sts.

Bind off loosely knitwise.

FINISHING

Wash and block if necessary. ■

Clara

DESIGNED BY WEI WILKINS

An airy scallop lace shawl is anchored by garter stitch edges
and elegant Chinese tassels at the ends.

FINISHED MEASUREMENTS
Approx 12½ x 53"/31.5 x 134.5cm after blocking

MATERIALS
- Two 3½oz/100g hanks (each approx 437yd/400m) of Cascade Yarns *Heritage Silk Paints* (superwash merino wool/mulberry silk) in #9817 water lillies
  Slight variations in color can occur with handpainted yarns, and can occur between dye lots.
- One pair size 4 (3.5mm) needles *or size to obtain gauge*
- Size F/5 (3.75mm) crochet hook
- Cardboard rectangle, 8"/20.5cm long, for tassels

GAUGE
28 sts and 36 rows to 4"/10cm after blocking over chart pat using size 4 (3.5mm) needles.
Take time to check gauge.

SHAWL
With crochet hook, chain 91. Place last st on knitting needle and pick up and k 90 sts through back of crochet chain—91 sts.

Begin chart
Row 1 (RS) K5, work chart to rep line, work 16-st rep 4 times, work to end of chart, k5.
Row 2 K5, work to rep line, work 16-st rep 4 times across, work to end of chart, k5.
Cont to work in this way, keeping first and last 5 sts of every row in garter st until row 12 is complete.
Rep rows 1–12 until piece measures approx 53"/134.5cm from beg, end with a row 12. Knit 1 row.
Bind off loosely.

FINISHING
Block to measurements.

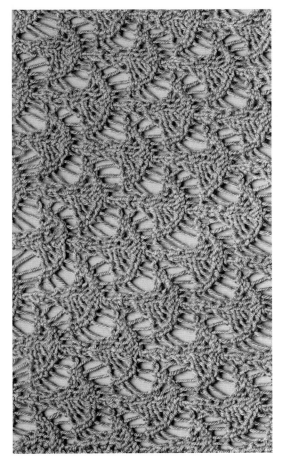

Tassels

Mark positions of 7 tassels at the points on each end of shawl. Wrap yarn around cardboard 12 times. Cut one end of looped yarn open. Draw the strands through a marked stitch to the halfway point so that ends are even. Wrap one end of an 18"/45.5cm length of yarn tightly around the top of the tassel 10 times, allowing the other end to form part of the tassel. Draw the wrapping end of the strand through the loop and pull both ends of the tying strand straight down. Neatly trim the tassel ends. ∎

STITCH KEY

☐ k on RS, p on WS

⊟ p on RS, k on WS

◿ k2tog on RS, p2tog on WS

◺ ssk on RS, p2tog tbl on WS

Ⓞ yo

⅄ S2KP on RS, sl 2, p1, psso on WS

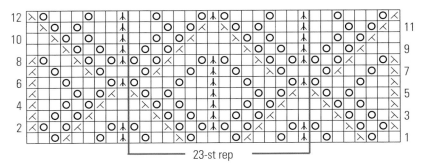

23-st rep

Lucille

DESIGNED BY NANCY TOTTEN

Increases and decreases shape chevron stripes and the ends are grafted together to form a modern, graphic infinity scarf.

FINISHED MEASUREMENTS
Circumference 45"/114cm
Width 8"/21.5cm

MATERIALS
- One 3½oz/100g hank (each approx 437yd/400m) of Cascade Yarns *Heritage* (superwash merino wool/nylon) each in #5632 plum (A) and #5649 iris (B)
- One pair size 2 (2.75mm) needles *or size to obtain gauge*
- Size C/2 (2.75mm) crochet hook and scrap yarn for provisional cast-on
- Stitch markers

GAUGE
40 sts and 40 rows to 4"/10cm over pat st using size 2 (2.75mm) needles.
Take time to check gauge.

PROVISIONAL CAST-ON
Using scrap yarn and crochet hook, chain the number of sts to cast on, plus a few extra. Cut the yarn and pull the tail through the last chain. With knitting needle and yarn, pick up and knit the stated number of sts through the "purl bumps" on the back of the chain. To remove scrap chain, when instructed, pull out the tail from the last crochet st. Gently and slowly pull on the tail to unravel the crochet sts, carefully placing each released knit st on a needle.

SCARF
With A, cast on 79 sts using provisional cast-on method.
Row 1 (WS) [K1, p1] twice, k1, place marker (pm), k to last 5 sts, pm, [k1, p1] twice, k1.
Row 2 (RS) [K1, p1] twice, k1, sl marker, ssk, k15, M1R, pm, k1, pm, M1L, k31, SK2P, k15, M1L, sl marker, k2, [p1, k1] twice.
Rep rows 1 and 2 for pat st, slipping markers every row, 17 times more.
Cont in pat st, working in color sequence as foll: *2 rows B, 20 rows A, 6 rows B, 10 rows A, 14 rows B, 6 rows A, 20 rows B, 2 rows A, 36 rows B, 2 rows A, 20 rows B, 6 rows A, 10 rows B, 14 rows A, 6 rows B, 20 rows A, 2 rows B*, 36 rows A, rep from * to *.
Work 1 row A.
Carefully remove provisional cast-on and place sts on free needle. Graft sts tog using Kitchener st and A. ■

Harriet

DESIGNED BY DORCAS LAVERY

The distinctive woven look of entrelac becomes even more eye-catching
with the striping effect of a variegated colorway.

FINISHED MEASUREMENTS
Circumference 23"/58.5cm
Length 6"/15cm

MATERIALS
- One 3½oz/100g hank (each approx 437yd/399.5m) of Cascade Yarns *Heritage Paints* (superwash merino wool/nylon) in #9770 celtic (1)
Slight variations in color can occur with handpainted yarns, and can occur between dye lots.
- Size 3 (3.25mm) circular needle, 24"/60cm long, *or size to obtain gauge*

GAUGE
28 sts and 34 rows to 4"/10cm over St st using size 3 (3.25mm) needles.
Take time to check gauge.

NOTE
Cowl is worked in the round when the base triangles are complete.

COWL
Cast on 110 sts loosely.

Base triangle
*Row 1 (WS) P2, turn.
Row 2 K2, turn.
Row 3 P3, turn.
Row 4 K3, turn.
Row 5 P5, turn.
Cont to work in this manner, working 1 additional st in each WS row, until row 15 *P10* is complete.
Do not turn.
Rep from * 10 times more—11 base triangles.
Tie the working yarn to the cast-on tail to form a round.

Tier one
Pick up and p 10 sts along edge of first base triangle, turn.
Next row (RS) Sl 1, k8, ssk (last st of rectangle with next st of base triangle), turn.
Next row P10, turn.
Rep last 2 rows until all sts of base triangle are used up, end with a RS row. Do not turn.
**Pick up and k 10 sts along edge of next base triangle, turn.
Next row (WS) P10, turn.
Next row Sl 1, k8, ssk (last st of rectangle with next st of base triangle), turn.
Rep last 2 rows until all sts of base triangle are used up, end with a RS row. Do not turn.
Rep from ** 9 times more—11 rectangles.

Tier two

Pick up and k 10 sts along the edge of the rectangle in the previous tier, turn.

Next row (WS) Sl 1, p8, p2tog (last st of rectangle with next st of next rectangle in previous tier), turn.

Next row K10, turn.

Rep last 2 rows until all sts of rectangle are used up, end with a WS row. Do not turn.

† Pick up and p 10 sts along the edge of the rectangle in the previous tier, turn.

Next row (WS) Sl 1, p8, p2tog (last st of rectangle with next st of next rectangle in previous tier), turn.

Next row K10, turn.

Rep last 2 rows until all sts of rectangle are used up, end with a WS row. Do not turn.

Rep from † 9 times more—11 rectangles.

Rep tier one and tier two once more, then rep tier one once.

End triangles

Pick up and k 10 sts along the edge of the rectangle in the previous tier, turn.

Next row (WS) P to the last st of end triangle, p2tog (last st of rectangle with next st of rectangle in previous tier), turn.

Next row K to the last 2 sts, k2tog, turn.

Rep last 2 rows until 3 sts rem, turn. P3tog, do not turn.

†† Pick up and p 10 sts along edge of next rectangle in previous tier, turn.

Next row (RS) K to last 2 sts, k2tog, turn.

Next row P to last st of end triangle, p2tog (last st of rectangle with next st of rectangle in previous tier), turn.

Rep last 2 rows until 3 sts rem, turn. P3tog, do not turn.

Rep from †† 9 times more—11 end triangles.

Fasten off. ■

Rosa

DESIGNED BY JACQUELINE VAN DILLEN

A tassel at the bottom plays up the shape of a triangular shawl
that elegantly combines cable and lace patterns.

FINISHED MEASUREMENTS
Width (along upper edge) 56"/142cm
Length (from neck to point) 24"/61cm

MATERIALS
- Two 3½oz/100g hanks (each approx 437yd/400m) of Cascade Yarns *Heritage Silk* (superwash merino wool/mulberry silk) in #5642 blood orange ❶
- Size 3 (3.25mm) circular needle, 40"/100cm long, *or size to obtain gauge*
- Cable needle (cn)
- Stitch markers

GAUGE
26 sts and 40 rows to 4"/10cm over charts 1 and 2 using size 3 (3.25mm) needle.
Take time to check gauge.

STITCH GLOSSARY
4-st RC Sl 2 sts to cn and hold to *back*, k2, k2 from cn.
4-st LC Sl 2 sts to cn and hold to *front*, k2, k2 from cn.

NOTE
Shawl is worked back and forth in rows from the point up. Circular needle is used to accommodate large number of sts. Do not join.

SHAWL
Cast on 4 sts. Work 12 rows in garter st (k every row).
Next row (RS) K4, pick up and k 6 sts along side edge, pick up and k 4 sts in cast-on edge—14 sts.
Next (set-up) row K4 (for garter st border), place marker (pm), p1 (for chart 2 pat), pm, p4 (for center cable), pm, p1 (for chart 1 pat), pm, k4 (for garter st border).

Begin charts
Row 1 K4, sl marker, work chart 1 to marker, sl marker, work chart 2 over next 4 sts (center cable), sl marker, cont chart 2 to next marker, sl marker, k4.

CHART 1

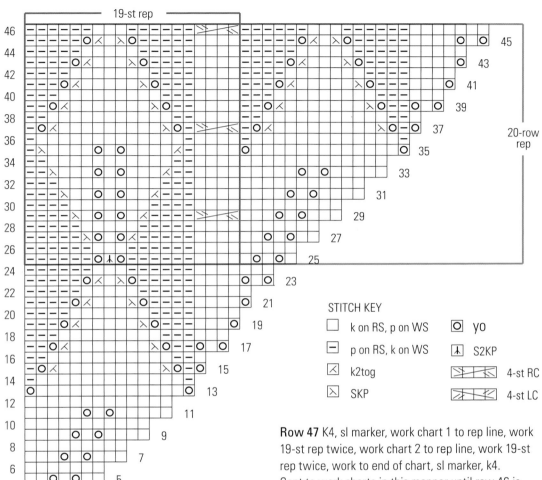

STITCH KEY

☐ k on RS, p on WS	⊙ yo
⊟ p on RS, k on WS	⋔ S2KP
⤢ k2tog	4-st RC
⤡ SKP	4-st LC

Row 47 K4, sl marker, work chart 1 to rep line, work 19-st rep twice, work chart 2 to rep line, work 19-st rep twice, work to end of chart, sl marker, k4. Cont to work charts in this manner until row 46 is complete. Rep rows 25–46 five times more, working one additional 19-st rep on each side of center cable every time the 22-row rep is complete. Then rep rows 25–42 once more—354 sts.

Begin chart 3
Next row K4, [work 4-st cable foll chart 1 as established, work the 15 sts of chart 3] 9 times, work center cable foll chart 2 as established, [work the 15 sts of chart 3, work 4-st cable foll chart 2 as established] 9 times, k4.

Row 2 K4, sl marker, work chart 2 to marker, sl marker, work center cable, sl marker, work chart 1 to next marker, sl marker, k4. Cont to work charts in this manner until row 46 is complete—94 sts. Rep rows 25–46 as foll:

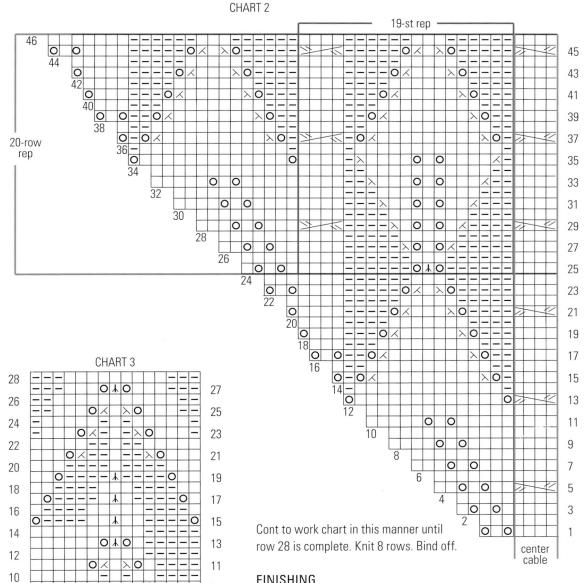

CHART 2

CHART 3

15 sts

Cont to work chart in this manner until row 28 is complete. Knit 8 rows. Bind off.

center cable

FINISHING
Block lightly to measurements.

Tassel
Cut 18 strands, each 8"/20.5cm long. Holding 18 strands tog, fold in half and draw loop through a st at the center point, draw ends through the loop and pull to tighten. Trim. ■

Coco

DESIGNED BY CHRISTINA BEHNKE

Daisy stitch and garter stitch alternate in a scarf that's a tale of texture.

FINISHED MEASUREMENTS
Approx 6½ x 62"/16.5 x 157.5cm

MATERIALS
- Two 3½oz/100g hanks (each approx 437yd/400m) of Cascade Yarns *Heritage Silk* (superwash merino wool/mulberry silk) in #5626 turquoise ❶
- One pair size 6 (4mm) needles *or size to obtain gauge*
- Stitch markers

GAUGE
20 sts and 32 rows to 4"/10cm over daisy pat using size 6 (4mm) needles. *Take time to check gauge.*

STITCH GLOSSARY
DS (daisy stitch) P3tog and leave on LH needle, yo RH needle and bring yarn to front between needles, p the same 3 sts tog and let drop from needle.

DAISY PATTERN
(multiple of 4 sts plus 3)
Row 1 (RS) Knit.
Row 2 P1, k1, *DS, k1; rep from * to last st, p1.
Row 3 Knit.
Row 4 *DS, k1; rep from * to last 3 sts, DS.
Rep rows 1–4 for daisy pat.

SCARF
Cast on 49 sts. Knit 3 rows.
Next (set-up) row (WS) K13, place marker (pm), k6, pm, k11, pm, k6, k13.

Begin pats
Row 1 (RS) K2, [work daisy pat to marker, sl marker, k to marker, sl marker] twice, work daisy pat to last 2 sts, k2.
Row 2 K2, [work daisy pat to marker, sl marker, p to marker, sl marker] twice, work daisy pat to last 2 sts, k2.
Rows 3 and 4 Rep row 1.
Rep rows 1–4 until scarf measures 61½"/156cm from beg, end with a row 2. Knit 4 rows. Bind off.

FINISHING
Gently steam block if necessary. ■

Sojourner

DESIGNED BY HALLEH TEHRANIFAR

A lace panel, textured rib pattern, and zigzag edges combine with a multicolor yarn to produce a scarf that's a feast for the eyes.

FINISHED MEASUREMENTS
Width (at widest point) 9¼"/23.5cm
Length 62"/157.5cm

MATERIALS
- Two 3½oz/100g hanks (each approx 437yd/399.5m) of Cascade Yarns *Heritage Silk Paints* (superwash merino wool/nylon) in #9801 fall foliage (■1)
  Slight variations in color can occur with handpainted yarns, and can occur between dye lots.
- One pair size 4 (3.5mm) needles *or size to obtain gauge*
- Stitch marker

GAUGE
23 sts and 33 rows to 4"/10cm over St st using size 4 (3.5mm) needles.
Take time to check gauge.

STITCH GLOSSARY
kfbf Knit into front, back, and front of stitch to increase 2 stitches.
k1b K1 in the row below.

FAGGOTING PANEL
(over 7 sts)
Row 1 (RS) K3, yo, k2tog, k2.
Row 2 K3, yo, k2tog, k1, kfbf.
Row 3 SK2P, k2, yo, k2tog, k2.
Row 4 K3, yo, k2tog, k2.
Rep rows 1–4 for faggoting panel.

TEXTURE RIB
(over an odd number of sts)
Row 1 (RS) [K1, p1] 5 times, k1.
Row 2 [K1, k1b] 5 times, k1.
Rep rows 1–2 for texture rib.

LACE PANEL
(over 13 sts)
Row 1 (RS) K3, [yo, k2tog] 3 times, k4.
Row 2 Knit.
Row 3 K4, [yo, k2tog] 3 times, k3.
Row 4 Knit.
Rep rows 1–4 for lace panel.

LACE EDGING
(beg with 18 sts; note that stitch count changes throughout)
Row 1 (RS) K9, [yo, k2tog] 3 times, yo, k3.
Rows 2, 4, and 6 Sl 1, k to last 7 sts, p7.
Row 3 K10, [yo, k2tog] 3 times, yo, k3.
Row 5 K11, [yo, k2tog] 3 times, yo, k3.
Row 7 P7, k5, [yo, k2tog] 3 times, yo, k3.
Rows 8 and 10 Sl 1, k to end.
Row 9 P7, k6, [yo, k2tog] 3 times, yo, k3.

Row 11 P7, k to end.
Row 12 [Sl 1, k1tbl, pass sl st over] 5 times, k to end.
Rep rows 1–12 for lace edging.

SCARF

Cast on 49 sts. Knit 1 row.
Row 1 (RS) Work faggoting pat over 7 sts, work texture rib over next 11 sts, work lace panel over next 13 sts, place marker, work lace edging to end.
Row 2 (WS) Work lace edging to marker, sl marker, work lace panel over next 13 sts, work texture rib over next 11 sts, work faggoting pat to end.
Cont in this manner, working pats and slipping marker every row, until scarf measures 64"/162.5cm from beg, end with a row 11. Bind off.

FINISHING

Block to open lace. ■

Dolley

DESIGNED BY MARI TOBITA

Garter stitch looks its prettiest in a sweet shawl worked from point to point with a lace edging and floral lace motifs.

FINISHED MEASUREMENTS
Wingspan 58"/147cm
Length at center back 14"/35.5cm

MATERIALS
- Two 3½oz/100g hanks (each approx 437yd/400m) of Cascade Yarns *Heritage Silk* (superwash merino wool/mulberry silk) in #5644 lemon ❶
- One pair size 5 (3.75mm) needles *or size to obtain gauge*
- Stitch markers

GAUGE
24 sts and 46 rows to 4"/10cm over garter st using size 5 (3.75mm) needles.
Take time to check gauge.

SHAWL
Cast on 4 sts.
Row 1 (inc RS) [K1, yo] twice, k to end—6 sts.
Row 2 and all WS rows Knit.
Row 3 Rep row 1—8 sts.
Row 5 (inc) [K1, yo] twice, k2tog, k to end—1 st inc'd.
Rep inc row every other row 3 times more—12 sts.
Row 12 (WS) K3, place marker A (pm), k to end.

Beg edging chart
Note Inc's are worked after marker A, every alternate 2nd and 4th row. Every 48 rows, 16 sts are added.
Row 1 (RS) Work chart row, sl marker, M1, k to end.
Row 2 K to marker, sl marker, work chart row.
Cont to work chart in this way, AT SAME TIME, M1 after marker A, every alternate 2nd and 4th row until row 16 is complete—18 sts.
Cont to inc in this manner and rep rows 1–16 twice more—28 sts.

Beg flower 1

Next (set-up) row 1 (RS) Work edging chart, sl marker A, M1, k3, k2tog, yo, k1, yo, ssk, k to end.
Row 2 Knit to marker, sl marker, work edging chart.
Row 3 Work edging chart, sl marker A, M1, pm E, work row 3 of flower chart over 13 sts, k to end.
Row 4 K to marker E, sl marker, k to marker A, sl marker, work edging to end.
Cont to work in this manner, working inc's every 2nd and 4th row as established, until row 16 of flower chart is complete.
Cont to work edging and inc's as established, work in garter st for 16 rows more.

Beg flower 2

Note Cont to work inc's every 2nd and 4th row after marker A. These inc's are not noted in pattern rows. When working stem rows, if there are an odd number of sts, it may be necessary to work a k1 after paired k2togs and yo's.
Row 1 (RS) Cont in pat as established to marker E, sl marker, work flower chart over next 13 sts, k to end.
Cont to work in this manner until row 6 of flower chart is complete.
Row 7 (stem row) (RS) Cont in pat to marker A, sl marker, *k2tog, yo; rep from * to marker E for stem, sl marker, work flower chart, k to end.
Cont to work in pats (without stem) until row 16 of flower chart is complete.

Beg flower 3

Row 1 (RS) Work in pats until 13 sts before marker E, pm D, work flower chart over next 13 sts, k to end.
Cont to work in pats, working stem on row 7 to marker D, until row 16 of flower chart is complete.

Beg flower 4

Row 1 (RS) Work in pat to marker E, sl marker E, work flower chart over 13 sts, k to end.
Cont to work in pats, working stem on row 7, until row 16 of flower chart is complete.

Beg flower 5

Row 1 (RS) Work in pat to marker D, sl marker, work flower chart over 13 sts, k to end.
Cont to work in pats, working stem on row 7 to marker D, until row 16 of flower chart is complete.

Beg flowers 6 and 7

Row 1 (RS) Work in pats until 13 sts before marker D, pm C; work flower chart over 13 sts, k to marker E, work flower chart over 13 sts, k to end.
Cont to work in pats, working stem on row 7 to marker C, until row 16 of flower chart is complete.

Beg flower 8

Work as for flower 5.

Beg flowers 9 and 10

Row 1 (RS) Work in pats until to marker C, work flower chart over 13 sts, k to marker E, work flower chart over 13 sts, k to end.
Cont to work in pats, working stem on row 7 to marker C, until row 16 of flower chart is complete.

Beg flowers 11 and 12

Row 1 (RS) Work in pats until 13 sts before marker C, pm B, work flower chart over 13 sts, k to marker D, sl marker, work flower chart over 13 sts, k to end.
Cont to work in pats, working stem on row 7 to marker B, until row 16 of flower chart is complete—82 sts.

Beg flowers 13 and 14

Note Discontinue inc's at this point and work even.
Row 1 (RS) Work to marker C, sl marker, work flower chart over 13 sts, work to marker E, work flower chart over 13 sts, k to end.
Cont to work in pats, working stem on row 7 to marker C, until row 16 of flower chart is complete.

Beg flowers 15 and 16

Row 1 (RS) Work to marker B, sl marker, work flower chart over 13 sts, work to marker D, work flower chart over 13 sts, k to end.
Cont to work in pats, working stem on row 7 to marker B, until row 16 of flower chart is complete.
Rep last 32 rows four times, then rep flowers 13 and 14 once more.

Beg flowers 17 and 18

Row 1 (RS) Work to marker A, sl marker, k2tog, k to marker B, sl marker, work flower chart over 13 sts, work to marker D, sl marker, work flower chart over 13 sts, k to end—1 st dec'd.
Cont in this way, working stem on row 7 to marker B, until row 16 of flower chart is complete, AT THE SAME TIME, dec 1 st after marker A every alternate 2nd and 4th row.

Beg flowers 19 and 20

Cont to dec as established after marker A, work 16 rows of flower chart after markers C and E, working stem row to marker C on row 7.

Beg flower 21

Cont to dec as established, work 16 rows of flower chart after marker D, working stem row to marker D on row 7.

Beg flowers 22 and 23

Work as for flowers 19 and 20.

Beg flower 24

Work as for flower 21.

Beg flower 25

Cont to dec as established, work 16 rows of flower chart after marker E, working stem row to marker E on row 7.

Beg flower 26

Work as for flower 21.

Beg flower 27

Work as for flower 25.
Cont to work edging chart and dec's as established, work 16 rows in garter st.

Beg flower 28

Work as for flower 25.
Cont in garter st, working dec's as established, work 16 rows of edging chart 3 times more—12 sts.

Next row (RS) Ssk, yo, ssk, k to end.
Next row Knit.
Rep last 2 rows 3 more times—8 sts.
Next row Ssk, yo, S2KP, k3—6 sts.
Next row Knit.
Next row Ssk, k2, k2tog.
Bind off rem 4 sts. ■

FLOWER CHART

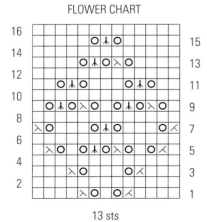

13 sts

EDGING CHART

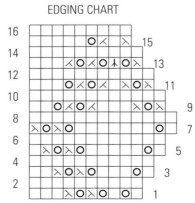

beg and end with 9 sts

STITCH KEY

☐	knit on both sides
⟋	k2tog
⟍	SKP
⊙	yo
⊼	S2KP

Marie

DESIGNED BY ANNA DAVIS

A drop stitch pattern pops in rich hues in a long cowl that's worked flat and seamed.

FINISHED MEASUREMENTS
Circumference 54½"/138.5cm
Length 8½"/21.5cm

MATERIALS
- One 3½oz/100g hank (each approx 437yd/400m) of Cascade Yarns *Heritage Silk* (superwash merino wool/mulberry silk) each in #5629 citron (A) and #5655 como blue (B) **1**
- Size 3 (3.25mm) circular needle, 47"/120cm long, *or size to obtain gauge*

GAUGES
28 sts and 38 rows to 4"/10cm over St st using size 3 (3.25mm) needles.
24 sts and 32 rows to 4"/10cm after blocking over drop st pat using size 3 (3.25mm) needles.
Take time to check gauges.

DROP STITCH PATTERN
(multiple of 10 sts plus 1)
Row 1 (RS) With A, knit. **Row 2** Knit.
Row 3 With B, *k6, [yo] twice, k1, [yo] 3 times, k1, [yo] 4 times, k1, [yo] 3 times, k1, [yo] twice; rep from * to last st, k1. **Row 4** Knit, dropping yos.
Rows 5 and 6 Rep rows 1 and 2.
Row 7 With B, k1, *[yo] twice, k1, [yo] 3 times, k1, [yo] 4 times, k1, [yo] 3 times, k1, [yo] twice, k6; rep from * to end. **Row 8** Rep row 4.
Rep rows 1–8 for drop st pat.

NOTES
1) Piece is worked back and forth in rows.
2) Carry color not in use loosely up the side of work.
3) Piece is worked with selvedge sts.

COWL
With A, cast on 323 sts. Do not join. Knit 2 rows.
Next row (RS) K1 (selvedge), work row 1 of drop st pat to last st, k1 (selvedge).
Cont in this way, knitting first and last st of every row, through row 8 of pat. Rep rows 1–8 six times more. With A, k 4 rows. Bind off loosely.

FINISHING
Block to measurements, extending dropped sts and allowing edges to scallop, if desired. Seam sides. ■

Sally

DESIGNED BY JACQUELINE VAN DILLEN

Sporty stripes are softened by a lace edging in a roomy
garter stitch shawl worked from point to point.

FINISHED MEASUREMENTS
Wingspan 52"/132cm
Length at center back 25"/63.5cm

MATERIALS
- One 3½oz/100g hank (each approx 437yd/400m)
  of Cascade Yarns *Heritage Silk* (superwash merino
  wool/mulberry silk) each in #5604 denim (A) and
  #5675 storm blue (B)
- Size 3 (3.25mm) circular needle, 24"/60cm long,
  or size to obtain gauge
- Stitch marker

GAUGE
24 sts and 44 rows to 4"/10cm over garter st using
size 3 (3.25mm) needles.
Take time to check gauge.

STRIPE PATTERN
Work 2 rows A, 2 rows B.
Rep these 4 rows for stripe pat.

NOTES
1) Shawl is worked from end to end and shaped with
increases and decreases.
2) Shawl is worked back and forth in rows. Circular
needle is used to accommodate large number of sts.
Do not join.
3) Stitch count changes within the chart pat.

SHAWL
With A, cast on 24 sts.

Begin chart and stripe pat
Row 1 (RS) With A, work chart row, place marker,
yo, k2—1 st inc'd.
Row 2 With A, k to marker, sl marker, work chart row
to end.
Row 3 With B, work chart row to marker, sl marker,
yo, k to end—1 st inc'd.
Row 4 With B, rep row 2.
Working body sts in garter st (k every row), cont to
work chart and stripe pat in this manner until row
16 is complete. Rep rows 1–16 for 14 times more—
144 sts.

Center back
Cont in chart and stripe pat as established.
Row 1 (RS) Work chart row to marker, sl marker, yo,
SKP, k to end.
Row 2 K to marker, sl marker, work chart row to end.
Cont to work even in this manner until row 16 is
complete. Rep rows 1–16 for 5 times more.

Beg decrease shaping

Next (dec) row (RS) Work chart row to marker, sl marker, yo, SK2P, k to end—1 st dec'd.

Next row K to marker, sl marker, work chart row to end.

Cont in pat as established and rep dec row every other row until the 16-row chart rep has been completed 15 times more—24 sts.

Bind off with A.

FINISHING

Block to open lace edging, pinning out the points. ■

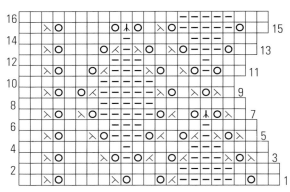

beg with 22 sts

STITCH KEY

☐ k on RS, p on WS

⊟ p on RS, k on WS

◿ k2tog

◺ SKP

⊡ yo

⊼ S2KP

Tools & Techniques

ABBREVIATIONS

approx	approximately	**M1 p-st**	make one purl stitch (see glossary)	**S2KP**	slip 2 stitches together, knit 1, pass 2 slip stitches over knit 1
beg	begin(ning)	**M1R**	make one right (see glossary)	**sc**	single crochet
CC	contrasting color			**sl**	slip
ch	chain	**oz**	ounce(s)	**sl st**	slip stitch
cm	centimeter(s)	**p**	purl	**spp**	slip, purl, pass sl st over
cn	cable needle	**pfb**	purl into front and back of a stitch—one stitch has been increased	**ssk (ssp)**	slip 2 sts knitwise one at a time, insert LH needle through fronts of sts and knit (purl) together
cont	continu(e)(ing)				
dec	decreas(e)(ing)				
dpn(s)	double-pointed needle(s)	**pat(s)**	pattern(s)	**sssk**	slip 3 sts one at a time knitwise, insert LH needle through fronts of sts and knit together
foll	follow(s)(ing)	**pm**	place marker		
g	gram(s)	**psso**	pass slip stitch(es) over		
inc	increas(e)(ing)	**p2tog**	purl two stitches together—one stitch has been decreased	**st(s)**	stitch(es)
k	knit			**St st**	stockinette stitch
kfb	knit into the front and back of a stitch—one stitch has been increased	**rem**	remain(s)(ing)	**tbl**	through back loop(s)
		rep	repeat	**tog**	together
k2tog	knit 2 stitches together—one stitch has been decreased	**RH**	right-hand	**WS**	wrong side(s)
		RS	right side(s)	**wyib**	with yarn in back
LH	left-hand	**rnd(s)**	round(s)	**wyif**	with yarn in front
lp(s)	loop(s)	**SKP**	slip 1, knit 1, pass slip stitch over—one stitch has been decreased	**yd(s)**	yd(s)
m	meter(s)			**yo**	yarn over needle
mm	millimeter(s)	**SK2P**	slip 1, knit 2 together, pass slip stitch over the k2tog—two stitches decreased	*****	repeat directions following * as indicated
MC	main color				
M1 or M1L	make one or make one left (see glossary)			**[ ]**	repeat directions inside brackets as indicated

SKILL LEVELS

Beginner
Ideal first project.

Easy
Basic stitches, minimal shaping, and simple finishing.

Intermediate
For knitters with some experience. More intricate stitches, shaping, and finishing.

Experienced
For knitters able to work patterns with complicated shaping and finishing.

METRIC CONVERSIONS

To convert from inches to centimeters, simply multiply by 2.54.

GAUGE

Make a test swatch at least 4"/10cm square. If the number of stitches and rows does not correspond to the gauge given, you must change the needle size. An easy rule to follow is: To get fewer stitches to the inch/cm, use a larger needle; to get more stitches to the inch/cm, use a smaller needle. Continue to try different needle sizes until you get the same number of stitches in the gauge.

KNITTING NEEDLES

U.S.	Metric	U.S.	Metric
0	2mm	9	5.5mm
1	2.25mm	10	6mm
2	2.75mm	10½	6.5mm
3	3.25mm	11	8mm
4	3.5mm	13	9mm
5	3.75mm	15	10mm
6	4mm	17	12.75mm
7	4.5mm	19	15mm
8	5mm	35	19mm

GLOSSARY

bind off Used to finish an edge or segment. Lift the first stitch over the second, the second over the third, etc. (U.K.: cast off)

bind off in rib or pat Work in rib or pat as you bind off. (Knit the knit stitches, purl the purl stitches.)

cast on Place a foundation row of stitches upon the needle in order to begin knitting.

decrease Reduce the stitches in a row (for example, knit two together).

increase Add stitches in a row (for example, knit in front and back of stitch).

knitwise Insert the needle into the stitch as if you were going to knit it.

make one or make one left Insert left-hand needle from front to back under the strand between last st worked and next st on left-hand needle. Knit into the back loop to twist the stitch.

make one p-st Insert needle from front to back under the strand between the last stitch worked and the next stitch on the left-hand needle. Purl into the back loop to twist the stitch.

make one right Insert left-hand needle from back to front under the strand between the last stitch worked and the next stitch on left-hand needle. Knit into the front loop to twist the stitch.

no stitch On some charts, "no stitch" is indicated with shaded spaces where stitches have been decreased or not yet made. In such cases, work the stitches of the chart, skipping over the "no stitch" spaces.

place marker Place or attach a loop of contrast yarn or purchased stitch marker as indicated.

pick up and knit (purl) Knit (or purl) into the loops along an edge.

purlwise Insert the needle into the stitch as if you were going to purl it.

selvage stitch Edge stitch that helps make seaming easier.

slip, slip, knit Slip next two stitches knitwise, one at a time, to right-hand needle. Insert tip of left-hand needle into fronts of these stitches, from left to right. Knit them together. One stitch has been decreased.

slip, slip, slip, knit Slip next three stitches knitwise, one at a time, to right-hand needle. Insert tip of left-hand needle into fronts of these stitches, from left to right. Knit them together. Two stitches have been decreased.

slip stitch An unworked stitch made by passing a stitch from the left-hand to the right-hand needle as if to purl.

work even Continue in pattern without increasing or decreasing. (U.K.: work straight)

yarn over Make a new stitch by wrapping the yarn over the right-hand needle. (U.K.: yfwd, yon, yrn)

STANDARD YARN WEIGHTS TABLE
Categories of yarn, gauge ranges, and recommended needle and hook sizes

Yarn Weight Symbol & Category Names	0 Lace	1 Super Fine	2 Fine	3 Light	4 Medium	5 Bulky	6 Super Bulky
Type of Yarns in Category	Fingering 10 count crochet thread	Sock, Fingering, Baby	Sport, Baby	DK, Light Worsted	Worsted, Afghan, Aran	Chunky, Craft, Rug	Bulky, Roving
Knit Gauge Range* in Stockinette Stitch to 4 inches	33–40** sts	27–32 sts	23–26 sts	21–24 sts	16–20 sts	12–15 sts	6–11 sts
Recommended Needle in Metric Size Range	1.5–2.25 mm	2.25–3.25 mm	3.25–3.75 mm	3.75–4.5 mm	4.5–5.5 mm	5.5–8 mm	8 mm and larger
Recommended Needle U.S. Size Range	000 to 1	1 to 3	3 to 5	5 to 7	7 to 9	9 to 11	11 and larger
Crochet Gauge* Ranges in Single Crochet to 4 inch	32-42 double crochets**	21–32 sts	16–20 sts	12–17 sts	11–14 sts	8–11 sts	5–9 sts
Recommended Hook in Metric Size Range	Steel*** 1.6–1.4mm Regular hook 2.25 mm	2.25–3.5 mm	3.5–4.5 mm	4.5–5.5 mm	5.5–6.5 mm	6.5–9 mm	9 mm and larger
Recommended Hook U.S. Size Range	Steel*** 6, 7, 8 Regular hook B–1	B–1 to E–4	E–4 to 7	7 to I–9	I–9 to K–10½	K–10½ to M–13	M–13 and larger

* Guidelines only: The above reflect the most commonly used gauges and needle or hook sizes for specific yarn categories.

** Lace weight yarns are usually knitted or crocheted on larger needles and hooks to create lacy, openwork patterns. Accordingly, a gauge range is difficult to determine. Always follow the gauge stated in your pattern.

*** Steel crochet hooks are sized differently from regular hooks—the higher the number, the smaller the hook, which is the reverse of regular hook sizing.

BASIC STITCHES

Garter stitch

Knit every row.

Circular knitting

Knit one round, then purl one round

Stockinette stitch

Knit right-side rows and purl wrong-side rows.

Circular knitting

Knit every round.

Reverse stockinette stitch

Purl right-side rows and knit wrong-side rows.

Circular knitting

Purl every round.

Seed stitch

Row 1 (RS) *Knit 1, purl 1, repeat from * to end.
Row 2 Knit the purl stitches and purl the knit stitches.
Rep row 2 for seed stitch.

KITCHENER STITCH (GRAFTING)

1. Insert tapestry needle purlwise (as shown) through first stitch on front needle. Pull yarn through, leaving that stitch on knitting needle.

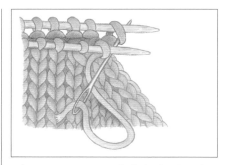

2. Insert tapestry needle knitwise (as shown) through first stitch on back needle. Pull yarn through, leaving stitch on knitting needle.

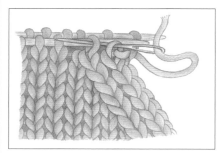

3. Insert tapestry needle knitwise through first stitch on front needle, slip stitch off needle and insert tapestry needle purlwise (as shown) through next stitch on front needle. Pull yarn through, leaving this stitch on needle.

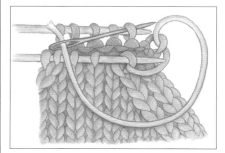

4. Insert tapestry needle purlwise through first stitch on back needle. Slip stitch off needle and insert tapestry needle knitwise (as shown) through next stitch on back needle. Pull yarn through, leaving this stitch on needle.
Repeat steps 3 and 4 until all stitches on both front and back needles have been grafted. Fasten off and weave in end.

CASTING ON

Long-tail cast-on

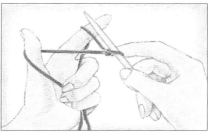

1. Make a slip knot on the right needle, leaving a long tail. Wind the tail end around your left thumb, front to back. Wrap the yarn from the ball over your left index finger and secure the ends in your palm.

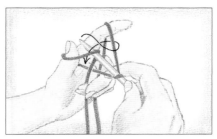

2. Insert the needle upward in the loop on your thumb. Then with the needle, draw the yarn from the ball through the loop to form a stitch.

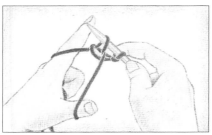

3. Take your thumb out of the loop and tighten the loop on the needle. Continue in this way until all the stitches are cast on.

Knitted cast-on

1. Make a slip knot on the left needle. *Insert the right needle knitwise into the stitch on the left needle. Wrap the yarn around the right needle as if to knit.

2. Draw the yarn through the first stitch to make a new stitch, but do not drop the stitch from the left needle.

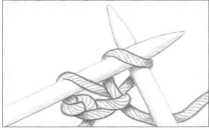

3. Slip the new stitch to the left needle as shown. Repeat from the * until the required number of stitches is cast on.

KNITTING WITH CIRCULAR NEEDLES

1. Cast on as you would for straight knitting. Distribute the stitches evenly around the needle, being sure not to twist them. The last cast-on stitch is the last stitch of the round. Place a marker here to indicate the end of the round.

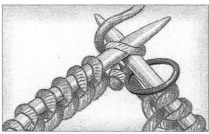

2. Hold the needle tip with the last cast-on stitch in your right hand and the tip with the first cast-on stitch in your left hand. Knit the first cast-on stitch, pulling the yarn tight to avoid a gap.

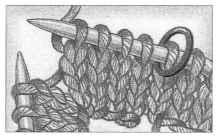

3. Work until you reach the marker. This completes the first round. Slip the marker to the right needle and work the next round.

KNITTING WITH DPNS (USING 4 NEEDLES)

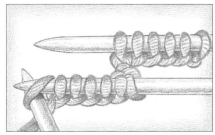

1. Cast on one-third the required number of stitches on the first needle, plus one. Slip this extra stitch to the next needle as shown. Continue in this way, casting on the remaining stitches on the last needle.

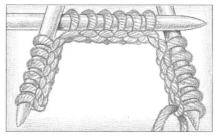

2. Arrange the needles as shown, with the cast-on edge facing the center of the triangle (or square).

3. Place a stitch marker after the last cast-on stitch. With the free needle, knit the first cast-on stitch, pulling the yarn tightly. Continue knitting in rounds, slipping the marker before beginning each round.

CABLES

Note: Cables shown are 6-stitch cables (3 sts on each side). Twists are made with 2 stitches (1 on each side). Stitch glossaries in each pattern specify stitch counts for cables used in that pattern.

Front (or left) cable

1. Slip the first 3 stitches of the cable purlwise to a cable needle and hold them to the front of the work. Be careful not to twist the stitches.

2. Leave the stitches suspended in front of the work, keeping them in the center of the cable needle, where they won't slip off. Pull the yarn firmly and knit the next 3 stitches.

3. Knit the 3 stitches from the cable needle. If this seems too awkward, return the stitches to the left needle and then knit them.

Back (or right) cable

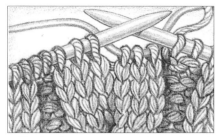

1. Slip the first 3 stitches of the cable purlwise to a cable needle and hold them to the back of the work. Be careful not to twist the stitches.

2. Leave the stitches suspended in back of the work, keeping them in the center of the cable needle, where they won't slip off. Pull the yarn firmly and knit the next 3 stitches.

3. Knit the 3 stitches from the cable needle. If this seems too awkward, return the stitches to the left needle and then knit them.

YARN OVERS

A yarn over is a decorative increase made by wrapping the yarn around the needle. There are various ways to make a yarn over, depending on where it is placed.

Between two knit stitches:

Bring the yarn from the back of the work to the front between the two needles. Knit the next stitch, bringing the yarn to the back over the right-hand needle, as shown.

Between a knit and a purl stitch:

Bring the yarn from the back to the front between the two needles. Then bring it to the back over the right-hand needle and back to the front again, as shown. Purl the next stitch.

Between a purl and a knit stitch:

Leave the yarn at the front of the work. Knit the next stitch, bringing the yarn to the back over the right-hand needle, as shown.

Between two purl stitches:

Leave the yarn at the front of the work. Bring the yarn to the back over the right-hand needle and to the front again, as shown. Purl the next stitch.

Multiple yarn overs (two or more):

Wrap the yarn around the needle, as when working a single yarn over, then continue wrapping the yarn around the needle as many times as indicated. Work the next stitch on the left-hand needle. On the following row, work stitches into the extra yarn overs, as described in the pattern. The illustration at right depicts a finished yarn over on the purl side.

FAIR ISLE STRANDING

One-handed

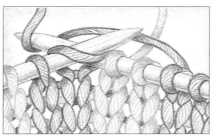

1. On the **knit side**, drop the working yarn. Bring the new color (now the working yarn) over the top of the dropped yarn and work to the next color change.

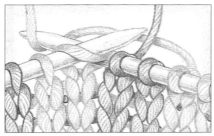

2. Drop the working yarn. Bring the new color under the dropped yarn and work to the next color change. Repeat steps 1 and 2.

1. On the **purl side**, drop the working yarn. Bring the new color (now the working yarn) over the top of the dropped yarn and work to the next color change.

2. Drop the working yarn. Bring the new color under the dropped yarn and work to the next color change. Repeat steps 1 and 2.

Two-handed

1. Hold the working yarn in your right hand and the non-working yarn in your left hand. Bring the working yarn over the top of the yarn in your left hand and knit with the right hand to the next color change.

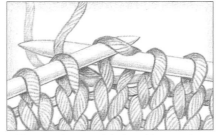

2. The yarn in your right hand is now the non-working yarn; the yarn in your left hand is the working yarn. Bring the working yarn under the non-working yarn and knit with the left and to the next color change. Repeat steps 1 and 2.

PICKING UP STITCHES

Along a horizontal edge

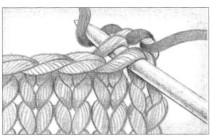

1. Insert the knitting needle into the center of the first stitch in the row below the bound-off edge. Wrap the yarn knitwise around the needle.

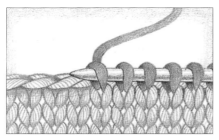

2. Draw the yarn through. You have picked up one stitch. Continue to pick up one stitch in each stitch along the bound-off edge.

Along a vertical edge

1. Insert the knitting needle into the corner stitch of the first row, one stitch in from the side edge. Wrap the yarn around the needle knitwise.

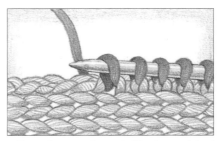

2. Draw the yarn through. You have picked up one stitch. Continue to pick up stitches along the edge. Occasionally skip one row to keep the edge from flaring.

With a crochet hook

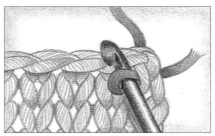

1. Insert the crochet hook from front to back into the center of the first stitch one row below the bound-off edge. Catch the yarn and pull a loop through.

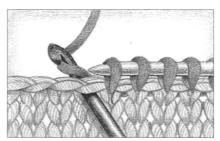

2. Slip the loop onto the knitting needle, being sure it is not twisted. Continue to pick up one stitch in each stitch along the bound-off edge.

SHORT ROW SHAPING: "WRAP & TURN"

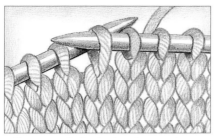

1. To prevent holes in the piece and create a smooth transition, wrap a knit stitch as follows: With the yarn in back, slip the next stitch purlwise.

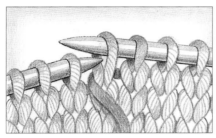

2. Move the yarn between the needle to the front of the work.

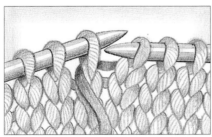

3. Slip the same stitch back to the left needle. Turn the work, bringing the yarn to the purl side between the needles. One stitch is wrapped.

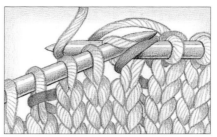

4. When you have completed all the short rows, you must hide the wraps. Work to just before the wrapped stitch. Insert the right needles under the wrap and knitwise into the wrapped stitch. Knit them together.

CHAIN STITCH (CROCHET)

1. Draw the yarn through the loop on the hook by catching it with the hook and pulling it toward you.

2. One chain stitch is complete. Lightly tug on the yarn to tighten the loop if it is very loose, or wiggle the hook to loosen the loop if it is very tight. Repeat from step 1 to make as many chain stitches as required for your pattern.

Index